DISCOVERING MARY

Answers to Questions About the
Mother of God

DAVID MILLS

SERVANT
BOOKS

PUBLISHED BY ST. ANTHONY MESSENGER PRESS
CINCINNATI, OHIO

Cover and book design by Mark Sullivan
Cover image: Petrov-Vodkin, Kuzma (1878-1939), The Mother of God.
Photo Credit : Scala / Art Resource, NY

LIBRARY OF CONGRESS CATALOGING-IN-PUBLICATION DATA
Mills, David, 1957-
Discovering Mary : answers to questions about the Mother of God / David Mills.
   p. cm.
Includes bibliographical references and index.
ISBN 978-0-86716-927-0 (pbk. : alk. paper) 1. Mary, Blessed Virgin, Saint—Miscellanea. 2. Catholic Church—Doctrines. I. Title.
BT603.M55 2009
232.91—dc22

2009022167

ISBN 978-0-86716-927-0

Published by Servant Books, an imprint of St. Anthony Messenger Press.
28 W. Liberty St.
Cincinnati, OH 45202
www.ServantBooks.org

Printed in the United States of America.

Printed on acid-free paper.

09 10 11 12 13 5 4 3 2 1

For Peter Toon, mentor, model and friend

CONTENTS

PREFACE

Three notes before we start.

First, I should thank the friends who read the manuscript and both caught mistakes and added insights of their own, for which they kindly let me get credit. Among them are Mike Aquilina, Cris Fouse, Frank Freeman, Anne Barbeau Gardiner, Renate Mross, Father David Poecking, William Tighe, David Wheeler-Reed, R.R. Reno and Father Jeffrey Whorton. Deserving of praise for several reasons, patience among them, is my editor, Cindy Cavnar, and my copy editor Lucy Scholand, whose exacting scrutiny and structural suggestions in particular improved the book.

Second, though the appendix gives a long list of recommended books, I should note several I found particularly helpful. Rereading the *Catechism of the Catholic Church* and the documents of the Second Vatican Council gave me a deep admiration for their wisdom and gratitude for the Church that produced them. The Marian essays in *The Encyclopedia of Early Christianity*, edited by Everett Ferguson, *The Catholic Encyclopedia* (available online at www.newadvent.org) and *Our Sunday Visitor's Encyclopedia of Catholic Doctrine*, edited by

Russell Shaw, gave useful surveys of the subjects and helped me put the particular matters in their context.

The *Dictionary of Mary*, Father Mateo's *Refuting the Attack Upon Mary*, Mark Miravalle's *Introduction to Mary* and Frederick Jelly's *Madonna* are all admirably well-written books that taught me a great deal. Dwight Longenecker's part of his and David Gustafson's *Mary: A Catholic-Evangelical Dialogue* gave an example of a thoughtful Catholic response to thoughtful Protestant objections. John Saward's *Redeemer in the Womb* showed me how much there is to learn and how beautiful are those truths.

And finally, this book is dedicated to a man who has been a beloved friend, a mentor, a teacher and an example, and who honored my wife and me by standing as the godfather of our third child. He was, as I wrote this, undergoing treatment for amyloidosis and facing it with admirable and convicting faith in our Lord. He died on the evening of April 25. I am blessed to be able to dedicate this book to Peter Toon and grateful beyond words to be able to commend him, in his illness and at his death, to the care and protection of Our Lady.

HOW I CAME TO LOVE OUR LADY

The seminary's chalice was made of clay, and predictably, someone eventually dropped it. A friend told me later that the pieces went straight into the trash.

I was appalled. This was a Protestant seminary, and I was not yet a Catholic, but I'd come to believe in something like the Catholic understanding of the Eucharist. That chalice had held the Lord, I thought, and someone treated it like a throw-away cup from McDonald's. *You don't do that.* (My colleagues believed that the wine was just a memorial, and that the real presence of the Lord was found not in the wine but in the people who shared the cup with each other—so who cares what you do with the pieces of the chalice?)

In my discovery of the Catholic Church, devotion to Mary came later than a lot of other discoveries, like realizing that God has given the Church a magisterium to guide it and learning to believe the priest when he says, "Behold, the Lamb of God," and believing my sins are forgiven as he pronounces the absolution when I'm sitting in that box at the back of the church. I didn't object to the Catholic Marian doctrines, as most Episcopalians did. I just didn't believe them. They thought them a denial of the gospel. I thought the content didn't matter one way or the other.

Marian devotion seemed to me the sort of thing that some people liked and others didn't but that no one had to practice. Some of it embarrassed me. It seemed a little too...Italian. It seemed to go along with loud excited conversation and baggy black dresses and the smell of garlic. It just wasn't me, who liked the white clapboard buildings and preppy clothes and simple solid food of the old New England town in which I grew up.

The Marian doctrines made perfect sense to me, and I rather enjoyed saying the Hail Mary (I was still close enough to my Protestant past for saying it to feel a little daring and racy), but I could not think of Mary in that personal, intimate way other Catholics did. I remember cringing, *after I became a Catholic*, when a woman I knew said, "I told the Blessed Mother..."

I had an easier time seeing my parish priest as a mediator than I did acting as if Mary were one. To talk of and to Mary as my Catholic friends did would have felt awkward and insincere, as if I were, at my age, playing army, creeping through our yard holding a stick and yelling "Bang!"

Dim, I know, but one comes to these things slowly. The Catholic tradition offers so much that the average convert picks it up in bits and pieces and may get an A in one subject and an F in another. I was getting at best a C- in knowledge of Mary and a D- in devotion to her. And I'm assuming that God is a generous grader.

The typical Catholic language really put me off, but that I assumed was just cultural: working-class Italian ladies and Irish laborers talk like that. (Episcopalians sometimes referred to the Catholic Church, only half-jokingly, as "the Italian mission.") I accepted the doctrines as a matter of faith when I came to believe the Catholic Church was who she said she was. The devotions I assumed I'd never adopt.

I had not yet learned that, in this as in so many other matters, you learn by doing. Only after being a Catholic for two or three years did I begin to understand why Catholics love Mary so energetically and why they speak to her so often. I first had to live a Catholic life. In particular I had to begin to understand the sacraments emotionally as well as intellectually, and really see and feel how God sanctifies matter.

DISCOVERING MARY

Most Protestants, including my former colleagues at the seminary, will say that Mary shows us how to respond to God, and some may call her the first and greatest of Christians (others won't), but for many her womb was merely the delivery system by which the Father brought His Son into the world. The virgin birth is important, but the Virgin herself isn't. After Jesus' birth Mary remained exactly the same as any other woman. I have heard Protestant friends of some academic and theological distinction say that in the list of great Christians, Mary falls well down the list, far below the apostles, the martyrs and even many modern missionaries.

I kind of thought that once. Though I intuited that she who bore the Word in her body had to be special somehow, I found it hard to justify my intuition. I could understand Mary as a model and as a distant subject of entreaty, but I could not relate to her as a mother, as *my* mother.

I knew that Catholics could appeal to Mary, that on becoming Catholic I was part of her family in a way I had not been before, I had a voice that would be heard. But I felt (as I see it now) that I had to do so rather like someone filling out a form and submitting it by mail to a high official, who was indeed noted for her benevolence but was still very far away. I never expected to meet her personally, any more than I expected to be invited to casual lunches at the White House to talk with the president.

Then, as I lived with the Church's sacraments, my heart changed. The curtains opened, the veil dropped, the static cleared. I began to feel the reality of the communion of saints in a way I never had before, actually to feel that our fathers in the faith are available to me and interested in my life, and I began to dimly understand something of what Mary's place in our salvation actually means and why Catholics speak of her and to her as they do.

I began to see how a sacred vessel is made holy by the sacred thing it carries. I began to *feel* this in a way I had not before. I found myself developing an experiential understanding of Mary and indeed a Marian devotion. Which surprised me. It surprised me *a lot*.

Having a model like Mary is a great thing, and having a benefactor in high places is even better, but having a mother (and a mother who is also a model and a benefactor) is a lot better. It allows fellowship, friendship, communion, not just imitation or entreaty. It is personal, not just moral or legal or economic. The way the Italian ladies talked soon made much more sense to me. I was learning to talk as they did, though without moving my hands so much.

I hadn't expected any of this. Discovering Marian devotion after you've entered the Church is a lot like getting another big present a week after your birthday.

And so I found myself, without really thinking about it, loving the vessel who held so great a thing as the incarnate God. I learned to speak to her without feeling self-conscious about it. I can't imagine thinking the way I used to, the love and the glory of Our Lady are so clear to me now.

And then I found out how much there was to know about Mary. I had thought, "Mother of God, conceived without original sin, assumed into Heaven, intercedes for us, to be praised, is the Mother of the Church, always points us to her Son—yep, got that taped." I remember reading about a theologian described as a "Mariologist" and wondering what he did the other 364 days a year.

I discovered that the Church has developed a great and subtle and complex understanding of Mary. What was at first glance a sparse description, contained in a few chapters of just two of the four Gospels, with a few short references in the other two, proved to be a rich source of understanding. The Church saw, for example, how various women in the Old Testament, and even the people of Israel taken as a body (when Israel is called "the daughter of Zion," for example), point to Mary and how those pointers tell us much more about Mary than the Gospels seem to tell by themselves.

The stories of the Nativity in Matthew's and Luke's Gospels are not independent stories, written down by a "just-the-facts" journalist. The birth of Christ was an event for which God had long prepared His people, including those who wrote the books that became our Old Testament, who without knowing it included pointers to Mary. The Nativity stories themselves were written by careful writers inspired by the Holy Spirit, who saw the pointers and constructed the stories so that we could see them too.

The Marian doctrines also proved far richer and more transformative—more directly relevant to my life—than I had ever thought. I had assumed that when you understand what the perpetual virginity of Mary means, you have understood everything you need to know, and that, anyway, it applies to Mary alone. I thought that when I learned that it has three parts to it, which I didn't know before I became a Catholic—the virgin conception, the virgin birth proper and the virgin life thereafter—I had finished the lesson and could turn the page.

But I then began to read more and saw that I actually had almost no idea what Mary's virginity means and why the Church has held to all three parts of the teaching so tenaciously. I had assumed it was mainly negative—mainly a way of telling the world that Jesus was the Son of God with extra force, because He did not have a father like the rest of us—and I suddenly started reading wise men and women who saw virginity as an active and transforming virtue and quality.

It included, for example, what has been called "the virginity of mind" and a "virginal disposition of soul," in the practice of which Mary could lead us. What that meant I did not know. But

I did see that the doctrine I'd thought abstract could help me change my life and bring me closer to God. There was vastly more here than had met my eye.

THIS BOOK

But I knew almost none of this when my family and I became Catholics, and for a few years thereafter. This book is the product of my growing to love Our Lady and therefore wanting to know a lot more about her, and finding out how grossly ignorant I was of the basic facts of her life and work.

When I was coming to know the young woman who would eventually become my wife, I found every little part of her story interesting: the name of her third-grade teacher, how she did in math in junior high, what books she loved and hated when she was little, what books she loved and hated now, where her family lived and what her room looked like and where they went to church and who she played with. We have been married twenty-six years now, and the pleasure such stories give me has not lessened. In fact I am thrilled when she comes up with a story I haven't heard.

That is the impulse I began to feel as I grew to love the mother of our Lord. I found, however, that all the Catholic books on Mary I could find tended to assume that you knew all the details and wanted something more theological or devotional. They were too rich for my blood, as the expression goes. It was a bit like trying to find out what atoms and molecules do and only finding books on quantum mechanics, or needing a glass of water after working for hours in the sun and being offered a fifty-year-old port. There wasn't much for us dullards.

And alas, I didn't hear much about her from the Catholics I knew or from the homilies at Mass, even on Marian feast days. She seemed to exist on the edge of things. When Catholics did speak about her, some of them seemed so worried about devotional "excesses" that they went out of their way to (so to speak) put her in her place. This struck me, as a newcomer, like the Secretary of Defense worrying about the dangers of enemies armed with crossbows. Excesses would be a sign of life.

I began collecting the details as I came across them, till an assignment from a Catholic newspaper, *Our Sunday Visitor*, gave me the chance to begin putting them in "FAQ" form. The exercise so helped me, ignorant as I was, that I thought a longer version would help others, not to mention helping me learn more. This book is the result.

It is not an apologetic work but a short guide to the basic facts, written for people like me. It does include some simple apologetic arguments and some analogies and illustrations, which I hope will be useful, but there is always much, much more to be said, even about the basics. I have found out something about atoms and molecules but leave physics to the experts. Other than providing a little explanation of my own, I have tried to say nothing in the book that is not either strictly factual or found in a magisterial document or in the work of a recognized expert in these matters, or commonly said among the faithful and learned people who write about these things.

In doing this I am not just avoiding subjects above my pay grade. I assume from observation that the best way into the subject for many people—cradle Catholics, prospective converts, new Catholics and Protestants interested in the subject alike—is through the facts we have in the common sources of Scripture and the Church's magisterial teaching tradition. We begin with the facts as a way to find the spirit of the thing—which when found helps us see more deeply into the facts.

If some of the answers seem obvious, I can testify from my own life that a writer writing on this subject cannot underestimate the possible ignorance of some of his readers. My ignorance was boundless. Vast. Embarrassing to remember.

I hope that the basics presented here will lead readers to study the subject of Mary more deeply. In her knowledge of the Mother of God, the Church has a great treasure, open for the taking. I am also hoping that readers find the information here not only interesting and useful but a way of deepening their devotion to the one who bore our Savior and deserves our love.

CHAPTER ONE

THE LIFE OF MARY

In the following I have tried to cover only the basics and present what might be called the common data on Mary's life. These are the plain cement blocks of the foundation, not the carved stonework of the mansion built on it.

The common data may seem unexpectedly sparse for someone as important in the Church's life and thought as Mary. Some critics have taken this to prove that the Church simply made up much of her Marian theology and devotion. They have offered many theories to explain why, like claiming that the Catholic vision of Mary is simply a Christianized version of the goddesses of the ancient world, or that devotion to Mary really expresses the desire of men who cannot relate to real women for an idealized and distant woman they can love. In any case, they say, it's all an illusion.

What the faithful Catholic finds, in fact, is that the basics prove almost infinitely suggestive, and not because theologians are inventive but because God's truth is deep and His revelation complex. The data are sparse only in the sense that the formula

"E=mc²" is short. One can take the story of Mary at the cross as a simple story of a son's provision for his mother, and it is that, but the Church has found in it all sorts of hints and clues as to the deeper meaning God, speaking through John, intended it to have.

The fact that John describes this scene at all, and that it takes place just before Jesus' death, is a hint; and Jesus' use of the title "Woman" in addressing His mother, as He did earlier at the wedding in Cana, is another; and His use of *hour* and s*pirit*, both words loaded with biblical meaning, is a third; and there are many others planted in the text. Wise and careful readers of Scripture have followed these hints and clues to the aspects and insights of the faith this apparently simple story contains.

Anyone who has learned the basics will want to go on, but even the basics of a subject like the life of the Mother of God are deep and rich and provide matter for a lifetime of reflection and prayer—not to mention a lifetime of imitation.

To the questions....

Where is the life of Mary described?

Primarily in Scripture, though the truths of her perpetual virginity and of her assumption into Heaven are given us clearly only in Sacred Tradition. The only explicit biblical information about Mary is given in the New Testament, of course, but the woman of whom God warns the snake in the story of the Fall (see Genesis 3:15) has been taken since the earliest Fathers to refer to Mary, and the "he" who will crush the serpent's head to Jesus. Although many saints have believed that Mary did not suffer pain in childbirth, even so the curse Eve receives in the next verse may apply to her, if it is taken to refer to the sword that will pierce her soul (prophesied by Saint Simeon in Luke 2:35) as she watches her Son suffer and die.

Mary is mentioned in six or seven books of the New Testament, depending on how Revelation 12 is interpreted (the great majority of theologians identify "the woman clothed in the sun" with Mary). About 150 verses can be called Marian verses, in which she is mentioned or involved, with almost two-thirds of those in Luke's Gospel.

Almost all the biblical information is given in the events in Jesus' life before He began His public ministry, starting with the Annunciation and ending with the twelve-year-old boy's return to Nazareth with Mary and Joseph after their trip to the temple for Passover. The Gospels tell just three stories of Mary's involvement in Jesus' public ministry, describing the wedding at Cana, Mary's visiting Jesus while He was preaching and her staying with Him as He died. John tells about the first and third, the other three Gospels about the second.

Mary is mentioned once in the Acts of the Apostles, staying with the apostles after the Ascension, once by Saint Paul, in his Letter to the Galatians, and possibly once in Revelation. More on Mary's place in Scripture is said in the next chapter, including an explanation of why someone so important isn't mentioned more often.

A number of apocryphal books from the early Church have offered more stories about Mary's life, both before and after the earthly life of her Son. They are not reliable sources for historical details, but they do witness to what Christians were thinking at the time, and some have influenced personal devotion and liturgical practices. The earliest and most famous of them is the mid–second-century work *The Protoevangelium of James*, which tells the story of Mary's early life and has sometimes been called "the gospel of Mary."

One story will give the flavor of the book and of the apocryphal sources in general. Mary has been living in the temple in Jerusalem, receiving food from "the hand of an angel," and when she turns twelve, God tells the high priest to gather all the widowers and He will show by a sign who should marry her. Nothing happens, and at the very end, as the high priest hands Joseph his staff, a dove flies out of it and lands on Joseph's head.

Are we sure the Mary described in the Bible existed at all?

Some skeptical writers—which include some famous Protestant theologians and biblical scholars, alas—have said that while Jesus obviously had a mother, everything or almost everything Scripture says about her is made up. The virgin birth they especially dismiss, insisting that Jesus had an earthly father because, well, all children have fathers.

These writers usually claim only to be using the objective methods of historians, which means that they write history as if God didn't exist. In fact they have a theological agenda of their own that requires eliminating the supernatural from the Gospels, which means essentially eliminating Mary, bearer as she is of so much that is obviously supernatural.

In the introductory note to this chapter I mentioned two ways these writers explain (and explain away) this inventiveness. In addition some claim that people have naturally been sentimental about Jesus and about motherhood in general and therefore have made up nice sweet stories about Jesus' mother. The stories are just folktales, they tell us, like those heart-tugging urban legends well-meaning friends send around by e-mail.

Christians have two responses to this claim.

First, the stories are part of the witness of Scripture as validated by the Church, and Christians believe that the Scriptures give us real history and that the Church has been careful to pass it on while weeding out the legends and myths. The rationality of trusting Scripture and the Church can't be argued here, but it is a perfectly reasonable commitment. You would trust a man you knew to be careful with details and scrupulous in reporting them when he tells you about his parents, especially when his stories hold together and fit what you know from other sources. This is more or less what the Christian does in trusting the Church and her Scriptures.

Second, the stories don't feel invented. They feel real. By this I mean that they do not show the signs of invention usual in religious literature of that age, pagan or Christian. Just compare the Gospels with the earlier mentioned *Protoevangelium of James*. There is a reason the Church endorsed the four Gospels and not these stories, even though the latter are more marketable, so to speak.

The scriptural stories are simple and unadorned, with rough edges that someone making up stories to celebrate Mary would have left out, like Jesus' rebuff when she comes to talk with Him, a story given in three of the Gospels. The description of

Mary suggests that it was an accurate account, because the average writer of the day would have made her look heroic. No one then could have conceived of a god born into such obscurity to such a poor guy in a backwoods town. The fact that there are so few stories also implies their accuracy, since a storyteller relying on his imagination would multiply the stories as well as the details. It is hard, for example, to imagine such a storyteller not making up an emotional story about Mary meeting Jesus during His Passion.

This is not courtroom evidence, of course, but it is enough to accept the scriptural stories as at least probably reliable accounts of historical events, even without a religious commitment. A betting man could safely bet on Mary's story being true.

Besides what Scripture tells us, can we guess anything about Mary's life?

The Church Fathers and Christians ever since have speculated on what Mary did and saw, given what the Scriptures say and what they knew of her place in God's plan of salvation. Why didn't she go to her Son's tomb with the other women, for example? Some have thought that she did not go with the other women to the tomb on Easter morning because she knew it would be empty. Having heard and seen all she had, from the visit of the angel Gabriel onward, she would have known that Jesus' death would not be final. We do not know if she knew this, but it is a sound guess that she did.

Did Mary see Jesus after His Resurrection? Similarly some, like the fourth-century Father Saint Ambrose, thought it obvious that Jesus appeared to His mother first after He rose from the dead: "Mary therefore saw the Resurrection of the Lord; she was the first who saw it and believed."[1] Pope John Paul II said something like this but more cautiously. Jesus, he said, may really have appeared first to Mary, noting her unexpected absence from the women who went to the tomb. The way he argues this gives a good example of the kind of careful speculation theologians have pursued. (The Fathers tended to speak rather definitively about such things, because that was the way people spoke of such things back then, while modern writers speak with more qualification.)

John Paul begins with a reasonable speculation from what the scriptural text says. To this exegetical argument he adds a theological one: Mary's presence at the cross and her perfect union with Jesus in His suffering "seem to postulate a very particular participation on her part in the mystery of the Resurrection." This participation implies that she, too, was "probably a privileged witness of Christ's resurrection, completing in this way her participation in all the essential moments of the paschal mystery." To this he adds another thought, based on what we know of the resurrection God has promised His people (see, for example, Romans 8:22 and Revelation 12): "Welcoming the risen Jesus, Mary is...a sign and an anticipation of humanity, which hopes to achieve its fulfilment through the resurrection of the dead."[2]

In the same way, some writers have seen in the Beatitudes (Matthew 5:1–12) a way of understanding the multiple meanings of Mary's title "blessed," given to her by the angel Gabriel and by Elizabeth and proclaimed by Mary herself in her prayer the Magnificat (Luke 1:46–55). The argument is simple and almost airtight: Mary is "blessed"; Jesus described blessedness this way; therefore Mary is blessed in the way Jesus described. Similarly, Jesus' declaration that those who hear God's Word and keep it are blessed (Luke 11:28) is applied to Mary as the perfect example of that obedience.

When was Mary born?

Scholars have made educated guesses, based on the Scriptures, the known history of the time, what we know of Jewish customs and the dating of Jesus' birth. If Jesus was born between 6 and 4 BC, as most scholars think, and she bore Jesus at fifteen or sixteen (as is commonly thought), she would have been born between 22 and 19 BC.

The Church celebrates her saints on their "birth" into Heaven, that is, on the day they die. Only Mary and Saint John the Baptist have their birthdays in the usual sense commemorated, as a sign that their entry into the world was part, and in Mary's case a crucial and necessary part, of God's plan for salvation. Mary's birth is celebrated on September 8, naturally enough nine months after the feast of her Immaculate Conception in the womb of her mother, Saint Anne.

When did Mary die?

We have no way of knowing or even guessing when Mary died. (If she did, that is; see below.) All we know is that she left the earth after the Ascension and presumably after Pentecost, because she is listed among those with the apostles in the beginning of Acts (1:14 and 2:1). If she was indeed fifteen or sixteen when Jesus was born, she would have been about fifty years old at Pentecost.

What does the name "Mary" mean?

Many scholars have studied and debated what the Hebrew name *Miryam* or *Miriam* means. Its meaning depends upon the languages and words from which it developed, which are not known for certain. Scholars have offered several possibilities, all closely related in meaning, among them "the exalted one," "the beautiful one" and "the perfect one." The full meaning might be a mixture of all of these.

This meaning, found using the standard tools of linguistics, makes sense theologically as well. The Christian presumes that God, who has (if I may put it this way) a sense of drama and form, would have ensured that the mother of His Son would have an appropriate name. He would have given us that sign or signal or hint.

Who were Mary's parents?

Tradition, deriving from the *Protoevangelium of James* and other apocryphal works, has named Mary's parents Joachim and Anne. In the *Protoevangelium* Joachim and Anne are said to be old and childless.[3] They are given a daughter miraculously, after an angel appears to Anne to tell her of the coming birth. Mary is their only child.

But whatever the historical value of the sources of information about Mary's parents, devotion to them was popular early in the Church's history, especially in the Eastern Church, while growing in the Western Church. Love for Mary naturally extended to love for her parents, who were, after all, Jesus' grandparents. Their cult was approved in the late sixteenth century.

Not surprisingly, various elaborate and fanciful stories have been told about Saint Joachim and especially about Saint Anne. A sixteenth-century writer, for example, held that Saint Anne's bearing of Mary was also a virgin birth, a view the Church condemned.

Despite the lack of information about Mary's parents, Christians have assumed that they must have been saints in order to raise the girl who would become the Mother of God. As the eighth-century Greek Father Saint John of Damascus, who is now a doctor of the Church, declared in a sermon:

> Joachim and Ann, how blessed a couple! All creation is indebted to you. For at your hands the Creator was offered a gift excelling all other gifts: a chaste mother, who alone was worthy of him. . . .
>
> Joachim and Ann, how blessed and spotless a couple! You will be known by the fruit you have borne, as the Lord says: *By their fruits you will know them.* The conduct of your life pleased God and was worthy of your daughter. For by the chaste and holy life you led together, you have fashioned a jewel of virginity. . . .
>
> Joachim and Ann, how chaste a couple!... While leading a devout and holy life in your human nature, you gave birth to a daughter nobler than the angels, whose queen she now is.[4]

The feast day of Joachim and Anne is July 26. The Church also celebrates their presentation of Mary in the temple on November 21.

Saint Anne is a patron saint of expectant mothers, women in labor, broom makers, equestrians and miners, as well as the Canadian province of Quebec, other occupations and places and many dioceses. Saint Joachim is a patron saint of fathers (along with Saint Joseph), grandfathers and grandparents (along with Saint Anne).

What about Mary's ancestors?

Of these we know nothing for certain, because the Bible does not give us Mary's genealogy. The two genealogies that Matthew's and Luke's Gospels give us are of Joseph's family. Through Joseph, Jesus is a member of the house of David, but the angel's statement to Mary that God will give her Son "the throne of his father David" (Luke 1:32) may mean that she was also of that family. In any case her marriage to Joseph would have brought her into the house of David, as a matter of Jewish law. Mary's ancestry may also trace back to the high priest Aaron, since Luke's Gospel tells us that her relative Elizabeth was "of the daughters of Aaron" (Luke 1:5).

What do we know about her husband, Saint Joseph?

Very little for certain. We have his genealogy (see Matthew 1:1–17, 20; Luke 3:23–38), and Luke's Gospel refers to his being a descendent of King David in explaining why he and Mary went to Bethlehem (Luke 2:4). We find out that he was a carpenter when Matthew relays the insults heaped on Jesus by the people of Nazareth after He taught in their synagogue (Matthew 13:55), though some scholars argue that the word used is closer to "master builder" than "carpenter." We know that he took care of Jesus at least until he was twelve and probably older, because "his parents" looked for Him when He remained in the temple in Jerusalem after Passover (Luke 2:41–51), after which the family returned to Nazareth and Jesus "was obedient to them" (Luke 2:51).

In 1870 Pope Pius IX named Joseph patron of the universal Church. His holy day, a solemnity (the highest sort of holy day), comes on March 19. It was introduced into the Roman calendar in 1479.

Joseph is also patron—the following is not a complete list, by any means—of several American dioceses (including Anchorage, Baton Rouge, Biloxi, Buffalo, Cheyenne, Hartford, La Crosse, Louisville, Nashville, San Jose, Sioux Falls and Wheeling-Charleston), of any number of dioceses and places around the world (including the nations of Bohemia, China, Korea, Mexico, Peru, Sicily, Vietnam and the city of Florence), of confectioners, wheelwrights, house hunters, and also those afflicted by doubt and hesitation. Not surprisingly, he is also a patron of fathers, families, married couples, chastity, cabinet-makers, carpenters, civil engineers, laborers, workers, travelers and unborn children. He is a patron of a holy death—fittingly, since he died in the company of Jesus and Mary. He was a patron of the Second Vatican Council.

He is also known as "Joseph the Worker" (his feast day under that title is on May 1) and "Joseph the Betrothed." In icons and other works of art, he almost always is shown with the child Jesus and usually with his tools.

Joseph has been the subject of much reflection by spiritual writers, including Saint Teresa of Avila, Saint Francis de Sales and Saint Bernadette. He has not been neglected in magisterial teaching. Pope Leo XIII offered a reflection "On Devotion to

Saint Joseph" in his encyclical *Quamquam Pluries* (1889), and on its hundredth anniversary, Pope John Paul II offered another, "On the Person and Work of Saint Joseph in the Life of Christ and of the Church," in his apostolic exhortation *Redemptoris Custos* (1989).

What kind of family and social class did Mary come from?

We don't know, except that her family would be the kind whose daughter would be betrothed to a carpenter or a master builder. That she and Joseph were not affluent is suggested by their offering two doves instead of a lamb at Mary's purification (see Luke 2:22–24). The family would perhaps have been what today would be called lower middle-class: supplied with the basics of life but with little for extras, and though employed in a field for which there is always demand, affected by changes in the economy.

Besides that, they lived in a small town—Nazareth wasn't even the main town in its area—in an unfashionable part of the country, in one of the Roman Empire's less valuable provinces. As we can see from the story of Peter's temptation, Galileans had a noticeable accent (see Matthew 26:73) and probably a kind of backwoods one.

That the Savior of the world came as the son of a lower middle-class woman from Nazareth may be an example of Saint Paul's observation that "God chose what is weak in the world to shame the strong" (1 Corinthians 1:27). It certainly tested the discernment of the people Jesus met: whether they saw the holiness or the background.

What do we know about Mary's religious practice?

We know that she and Joseph were religiously serious and observant Jews. Not only did they have Jesus circumcised and present Him in the temple, following the Jewish law, but Luke tells us that they went to Jerusalem for the Feast of Passover every year (see Luke 2:41), no small investment of time and money. Because we know of Mary's extraordinary obedience to God, we can assume her obedience to the authorities God had given His people and her adherence to the rites and ceremonies of the Jewish religion.

Did Mary have other children after Jesus?

No. The Church teaches that Mary bore only one child and, indeed, that she remained a virgin. The perpetual virginity of Mary is an ancient teaching of the Church, which is held also by the Orthodox Churches and was even held by the major Protestant reformers in the sixteenth century.

The references to Jesus' brothers in the Gospels and Acts (in Matthew 12:46 and Acts 1:14, for example) are held to refer to step- or foster brothers, cousins or other relatives. There is no reason in the text to assume that it means "brothers" in our sense, as the word often refers to relatives (see Genesis 14:14; Ruth 4:3; 2 Samuel 17:25 for examples). The James and Joseph referred to at one point in Matthew as Jesus' brothers seem to be the same James and Joseph that are later identified as the sons of another woman (Matthew 13:55 and 27:56).

Some believe that Joseph was a widower with children when he married Mary, so these "brothers" were actually stepbrothers, and others have argued that they were foster brothers. Whatever the truth of the matter, and we haven't been told it, the Church teaches firmly and—the sources suggest—from the beginning that Mary had no more children after Jesus.

The Church's belief is sometimes attacked by Protestant writers, who insist that *brothers* must mean "other children of Mary." One biblical argument against this—and there are others—is the story of Jesus' committing His mother to His disciple Saint John. This would have been a crime against tradition if she had had another child to take care of her. In any case the Protestant critic would have to admit that the biblical evidence is unclear and that his criticism is as much a product of a doctrinal assumption as he believes the Catholic's commitment to be.

This question will be taken up in more detail in chapter three, on Church doctrine.

Wouldn't Joseph have wanted more children?
The Scriptures do not tell us, and there is no official teaching on the matter, but almost certainly not. The man God prepared to be Mary's husband and to raise the child Jesus would be a man intent on doing the will of God. He would, as many writers have said, be a saint nearly as extraordinary as Mary herself. He would never have wanted to violate that continuing virginity of Mary that God willed.

And though this is admittedly pure speculation, it is hard to imagine a man, especially a great saint, given the task of raising the incarnate Son of God and taking care of His mother, wanting to fill the house with other children. In the same way someone might put a family treasure in a single frame or setting, because it is not only special but unique, so a man like Joseph might set a woman like Mary and a boy like Jesus.

His instinct in this may well have been like our own instinct for the separation of liturgical vessels that hold the Body and Blood of the Lord: We feel that any secondary use of these vessels would defile them. Not that the secondary use is bad in itself, but it is wrong for these particular vessels. Something of this attitude toward holy things was already part of Jewish spirituality, as seen in the restrictions on the priesthood (see Leviticus 21:1–24). The devout Joseph would have known that Mary was a sacred vessel.

Did Mary have an extended family?

This is another matter on which we have no information, but some scholars have said that the Bible's use of the word *brothers* for cousins and others suggests an unusually close extended family. It is possible that many of them lived with Jesus, Mary and Joseph, perhaps after the death of their parents. That some "brothers" remained with the apostles after the Ascension—that they remained loyal to the end—may suggest this as well.

Some scholars have also suggested that the story of the Holy Family's return from celebrating the Passover in Jerusalem (see Luke 2:41–51) implies that Mary or Joseph had a big extended family or clan. This would explain why they did not notice that Jesus was missing for an entire day. Luke tells us that they "suppose[d] him to be in the company," which could imply other family members in a long train of people.

Did Mary have a choice whether to be the mother of Jesus? Could she have said no?

Mary had a choice, because God the Father would never override someone's freedom, and certainly not in giving His Son a mother. But immaculately conceived and free from sin, she would freely choose to do God's will. That the choice was inevitable, given Mary's character, does not mean it was not free. Her "Let it be to me according to your word" (Luke 1:38) was a perfectly free act and yet a perfectly predictable one. Mary was doing what she wanted to do, because she *wanted* to do whatever God asked of her.

This may explain what seems like an odd feature of the story of the Annunciation: the angel declares to Mary what God would do but still waits for her answer. The declaration is made in confidence, but the answer is still awaited. Here again Mary shows us both what we ought to be and what we shall be: creatures who in perfect freedom choose God.

How do we know about the virgin birth, the visit of the Magi and the other events of Jesus' childhood?

Probably through Mary herself, though Matthew and Luke could have had other sources. The story of the Annunciation, for example, could have come from someone else in the room—Saint Anne being an obvious possibility or Gabriel himself—or from knowledge given supernaturally to Luke to help him write the story God wanted him to write. While asserting the inspiration of Scripture, the Church makes no claims about the origins of the biblical stories. But that Mary told others what had happened is the simplest explanation.

This might help explain the Gospels' relative lack of information about Mary. She might have downplayed her own role and urged others to say only about her what they needed to say in order to speak more fully about Jesus. This is only a guess, but it fits what we know about Mary, and what we know about mothers.

The Gospels and Acts tell us that Mary sometimes visited Jesus during His public ministry (and may well have traveled with Him), that she stayed with the apostles after the Crucifixion and that she was in John's care after Jesus' Ascension. The earliest followers of Jesus would naturally have asked her many questions about the life of their Lord, and new converts would have been pointed to her as the mother of the man the apostles were proclaiming. Anyone wanting to write a biography of Jesus—Matthew, Mark, Luke and John, say—would have talked to her or gotten her stories from someone who had.

The stories of Mary's life and Jesus' youth—undoubtedly a great many more stories than have come down to us—would have been the common possession of the early Church. This helps explain why some truths the Church proclaims in her liturgy and calendar cannot be found directly expressed in Scripture, a subject we will look at more in the next chapter.

Mary's continued virginity, for example, would have been part of the early Christians' common knowledge, but as the matter did not arise in the course of writing the works that became the New Testament, the writers would not have said anything about it. Saint Paul, for example, was writing particular people with particular problems, not giving them a comprehensive course in Christian teaching. That course he had certainly given them when he evangelized them, and he did not need to repeat it in his letters.

It is hard to think of anyplace in the New Testament where the subject of Mary's virginity would naturally come up. For that matter, Scripture doesn't tell us that neither Jesus nor Saint Paul married, but everyone knows they didn't, that fact being part of the uninterrupted common knowledge of the Church.

Something like this might happen today. A collection of theologically oriented essays on the life and work of Pope John Paul II might tell the story of his youth in Poland but leave out his continuing love for his homeland and his involvement in its life after he became pope. The writers would be focused on explaining his theology of the body, summarizing his encyclicals and describing the development of his thinking on Mary. They would all know how much he loved Poland and how he helped in its liberation from communism, and they would all assume the readers knew this as well, so they might never mention it.

They would assume that others would pass on such information. It would not be untrue even if we never saw it in writing but heard it from a friend, who'd heard it in a sermon preached by a priest who had been taught it by his bishop, who learned it while visiting the Vatican from someone who'd known John Paul II.

Why was Jesus born of a Virgin?

As with many events in the life of Christ, the Church's official teaching has been more concerned to assert the fact of the virginal conception and birth of our Lord than to explain it. The

Church believes that God had His reasons for having Him be born as a child of a virgin mother, and we may be able to intuit some part of them, but it happened whether or not we can guess those reasons. Catholics are free to speculate, but the Church's Scripture, teaching, and liturgical life, all drive us back to the fact itself, a matter primarily for assent, wonder and adoration.

The early Fathers and the earliest creeds all speak insistently of Mary as "the Virgin." Speaking in the same way as the Fathers, the Second Vatican Council's Dogmatic Constitution on the Church, *Lumen Gentium*, insists upon Mary's virginity, and repeatedly uses "Virgin" as a title, but says nothing about the reason for it. The American bishops, in their pastoral letter on Mary, *Behold Your Mother*, note that in the virgin birth God has intervened in a "unique way" and offered mankind "a fresh start." The most they will say is that it is "the sign that the Incarnation is the new creation, independent of the will of man or urge of the flesh (Jn 1:13)."[5]

Beyond that we have some hints from Church teaching that Mary's virginity symbolizes the fundamental Christian orientation to the world. One is that the Virgin Mary, as Mother of the Church, models for us a virginal life as not just a limitation or a sacrifice but also an active and transformative power. As *Lumen Gentium* put it,

> By preaching and baptism she [the Church] brings forth sons, who are conceived of the Holy Spirit and born of God, to a new and immortal life. She herself is a virgin, who keeps in its entirety and purity the faith she pledged to her

spouse. Imitating the mother of her Lord, and by the power of the Holy Spirit, she keeps intact faith, firm hope and sincere charity.[6]

One reason modern Americans may have trouble answering this question is our decadent view of virginity. For us the question tends to be, "Why not have intercourse?" Virginity is a loss. For Mary and for the consecrated virgins since her, it may be a sacrifice, but it is also a power and a glory.

How close was Mary to Jesus after He began His public ministry?

Given who Mary knew Jesus to be, a matter that she meditated upon (see Luke 2:19), she would have followed His ministry closely, though whether she traveled with Him we do not know. The Gospels suggest that she sometimes heard Him speak (as revealed in the story told in Matthew 12:46–50, Mark 3:31–35 and Luke 8:19–21), and of course they were together at the wedding in Cana (John 2:1–12), where, at His mother's request, Jesus performed His first miracle.

They may well have met in Jerusalem at Passover, since the Gospels imply that Jesus went every year, and Mary may well have continued her practice of going every year as well. She was in Jerusalem for Jesus' final Passover and saw him crucified (see John 19: 25–27).

Was Mary a witness to the Resurrection?

Scripture does not include Mary in its list of witnesses to Jesus' Resurrection, but it does not exclude her either. Some writers have, as I've mentioned, suggested that she did not go to the tomb because she knew it would be empty. It is hard to believe Jesus would not have seen His mother, when He took such care to arrange for her future well-being even while dying in agony. But we don't know for sure that He did.

What did Mary do after the Ascension?

Acts tells us that she remained with the apostles and joined them in their prayers, before the story moves on to tell of the missionary expansion of the early Church. As far as we can tell, since she was in John's care, she was with the apostles at Pentecost. *Lumen Gentium* tells us that she helped the Church at its beginnings by her prayers, noting that she asked for "the gift of the Spirit, who had already overshadowed her in the Annunciation."[7]

There is also a theological reason for assuming Mary to have been with the apostles at Pentecost. The Holy Spirit had overshadowed her at the Annunciation. Her presence on Pentecost, now seeing the new Church overshadowed as well, would tie together Jesus and the Holy Spirit, emphasizing that the Spirit is the Spirit of Christ and that any spirit who does not honor the Lord come in the flesh is a false spirit (see 1 John 4:2–3). Her presence would be a sign that the Church as the body of Christ really is the continuing presence of the Christ she bore.

An ancient tradition tells us that Mary stayed in Jerusalem for a long time, another (not necessarily contradicting the first) that she and John went to live in Ephesus where, following Jesus' instructions, they lived as son and mother. We don't know anything else about her life after Pentecost until her Assumption into Heaven.

Did Mary die?

Scripture does not tell us, and the Church has never said in any magisterial statement whether Mary died or went to Heaven without dying, as had Enoch (see Genesis 5:24) and Elijah (2 Kings 2:11–12). When Pope Pius XII declared belief in her assumption a dogma in 1950, the declaration said only that by her immaculate conception "she was not subject to the law of remaining in the corruption of the grave" and that "having completed the course of her earthly life," she "was assumed body and soul into heavenly glory."[8] This way of putting it was chosen intentionally.

Some have said that she did not die, arguing that her immaculate conception freed her from death, since death was the result of original sin. The great majority of Christian writers since the fourth and fifth centuries have said that Mary died. The Eastern Christian tradition—which includes both the Eastern Catholic Churches faithful to the pope and the Orthodox Churches—teach the "dormition," or falling asleep, of Mary.

What happened to Mary when she died (if she did)?

The Catholic teaching is that Mary was taken up, or "assumed," into Heaven "body and soul." There she reigns as the Queen of Heaven, the feast of which the Church celebrates on August 22, at the end of the octave of the Feast of the Assumption on August 15. This is addressed more fully in chapter three, on doctrine.

CHAPTER TWO

MARY IN THE BIBLE

This chapter surveys the information about Mary given us in Scripture. As in the preceding chapter, I have stayed with the common data, the facts and truths that anyone reading the Bible carefully with the mind of the Church will find. I have a reason for this, besides caution in treating a matter of such importance and such subtlety, not to mention one on which many have strong views.

As the American bishops wrote in their pastoral letter *Behold Your Mother*, the "approach to the Virgin Mary based on the Bible is especially suited to the needs of our day."[1] This is true in part because the first question many of us who have come to the Church from the outside ask is not "What does this mean?" or "Is this true?" but "Just *where* did they get this?" We want to know that the foundation from which the Marian teaching is developed is sound and secure. The Marian teaching is so new to us that we want to check its birth certificate.

A degree of suspicion is not unreasonable. Some books and articles on Mary find in the biblical stories more than they contain, even when the writers are trying only to explain what the passages mean. The readings are almost always perfectly plausible, and often quite likely, but nevertheless not what the text actually says.

Some writers, for example, declare that the inclusion of Mary in the list Acts gives of the people gathered together after the Ascension (Acts 1:14) shows her at the center of the Church, nurturing the apostles and being a mother to the early Church as she had been to the Son of God. That she was the Mother of the Church in a direct and personal way to those early believers who knew her is quite likely, indeed almost certain, but that one verse in Acts does not actually say this. It is an educated guess, not a summary.

Reading too much into Scripture avoids a fruitful wrestling with Scripture and directs our attention away from the Church's other reasons for her teaching about Mary. The Catholic Church has a great gift in her living tradition and in the subtle interplay and mutual support of Sacred Scripture and Sacred Tradition, and she need not stretch one to find in it a truth given more fully in the other. (We will take this up again in the next chapter.)

Indeed, what strikes the newcomer who looks closely at the Church's teaching is what might be called her exegetical chastity: the Church's care not to say too much, to establish first what Scripture tells us directly and second what may rightly be read into Scripture, between the lines, so to speak, and to distinguish these insights from what may be plausible and edifying but is not certain. This kind of reading—obedient to one's vocation as a reader, submitted to the Word, treasuring what is given, careful to say nothing of one's own but to point to the message itself—might indeed be called Marian.

Where is Mary talked about in the New Testament?

Mary is mentioned in the four Gospels, the beginning of the Acts of the Apostles, in one verse in Paul's Letter to the Galatians, and in Revelation, if the "woman" described in chapter 12 is taken to be Mary.

|+|Matthew's Gospel begins with Jesus' genealogy through Joseph, mentioning Mary at the end (1:16) and pointedly declaring that of her was born the man called the Messiah or Christ. It stresses Jesus' membership in the Jewish people.

Then begins the story of Jesus' early life: His birth (1:16, 18–25), the visit of the Magi (2:1–12), the Holy Family's flight into Egypt and King Herod's attempt to kill the newborn King by killing all the young boys in Bethlehem, called the slaughter of the innocents (2:13–18), and the Holy Family's return to Nazareth after Herod dies (2:19–23). Mary is mentioned only one more time, when she and Jesus' "brothers" (meaning cousins or relatives, as we discussed in the first chapter) come to Jesus (12:46–50), a story also told in Mark and Luke.

|+|Mark's Gospel begins not with the story of Jesus' birth but with the preaching of Saint John the Baptist, preparing the people for Jesus, and then Jesus' Baptism. The two times Mary is mentioned are in the encounter of Jesus with his "brethren," where she appears as Jesus' mother but is not named (3:31–35), and in the quotation from the people of Nazareth who, both astonished at and offended by Jesus' teaching in their synagogue, ask, "Is not this the carpenter, the son of Mary?" (6:3).

|+|Luke's Gospel begins with the story of the conception of Saint John the Baptist. It proceeds with the story of the Annunciation (1:26–38), followed by the pregnant Mary's visit to her relative Saint Elizabeth (1:39–56), which includes the prayer of praise Mary offered that we call the Magnificat. After describing the birth of Saint John the Baptist, the Gospel describes the birth of Jesus (2:1–7), the visit of the shepherds (2:8–20) and then the Holy Family's participation in two important rituals, Jesus' circumcision (2:21) and his presentation in the temple (2:22–38). The story of the circumcision tells of the first time Jesus shed blood for man, and the story of the presentation gives us the prayer of Saint Simeon we call the *Nunc Dimittis* and his prophecy that Mary's soul would be pierced by a sword.

Luke then tells the only story we have of Jesus' youth (2:41–50). The twelve-year-old Jesus remained in the temple in Jerusalem after Passover and had a learned discussion with the teachers there, amazing everyone who heard it. In the end He tells His worried mother that she should have known He would be in His Father's house.

Luke ends this story with Jesus' returning home to Nazareth with Mary and Joseph and obeying them, and with the closing note that Mary "kept all these things in her heart" (2:51). (By the way, we might guess something of the nature of the Holy Family's home life in some of the stories of family life that Jesus told in his preaching and teaching—Luke 11:11, for example—though he also understood the other side, as he showed in the story of the prodigal son in Luke 15:11–32.)

The final verse of this passage, covering the period some-times called "the hidden life of Jesus," gives a transition to Luke's exposition of Jesus' public ministry: "And Jesus increased in wisdom and in stature and in favor with God and man" (2:52).

This Gospel offers its genealogy of Jesus (3:23–34) only when it begins describing Jesus' public ministry, and in contrast to Matthew's genealogy, it stresses Jesus' universality. Luke mentions Mary only once more, in the story his Gospel shares with Matthew's and Mark's (8:19–21), though she may well have been among the women who later went to Jerusalem with Jesus (23:55).

|+| John's Gospel begins with a theological prologue describing the incarnation of the eternal Word (1:1–18), which does not mention Mary directly but does declare that "the Word became flesh" (1:14), an obvious allusion to the mother through whom He became man.

The first time Mary is mentioned by name is in the story of the wedding at Cana, where at her request Jesus performs His first miracle, turning water into wine (2:1–11). The miracle at Cana is not only the first but one of only seven miracles recorded in this Gospel. It also contains the last words of Mary that the Bible gives us, significantly enough, "Do whatever he tells you" (2:5).

The second mention of Mary is the story of her at the cross (19:25–27). There Jesus places her in John's care.

In both stories Jesus calls His mother "woman," which sounds to our ears slightly rude. In no place in Greek literature or the Septuagint (the Greek version of the Old Testament) does a son address his mother this way. John seems to have meant his readers to think of Mary in relation to Eve, or rather in contrast to Eve.

|+| In the Acts of the Apostles, Mary appears only once: She is one of those who remained with the apostles after Jesus' Ascension and devoted themselves to prayer (1:13–14). Here she is both mentioned by name, as are the apostles but not the women or Jesus' "brethren," and identified as the mother of Jesus. It is almost certain that Mary was among those gathered when the Holy Spirit descended at Pentecost (2:1–4), especially as she would have remained with John, in whose care Jesus had placed her.

|+| In all his letters Saint Paul mentions Mary just once, though not by name, and does so in declaring to the Galatian Christians the effect and the reward of faith in Christ. He tells about the Son "born of woman, born under the law" (4:4) so that we could become God's sons and heirs through adoption. This is the first time Mary is mentioned in a book of the New Testament, Galatians being written well before the Gospels.

|+| Finally, the woman "clothed with the sun" (an image taken from Genesis 37:9) that Saint John sees in the vision recorded in Revelation 12 is identified by most biblical scholars and theologians (John Paul II among them) with Mary. The traditional reading favors identifying the woman with Mary. Pope Saint Pius X said, for example, "Everyone knows that this woman

signified the Virgin Mary, the stainless one who brought forth our Head," and John Paul II said something similar, while Pope Paul VI said a little more reservedly that the passage "is interpreted by the sacred Liturgy, not without foundation, as referring to the most blessed Mary."[2]

The sides argue partly about whether the details can all refer to Mary, especially the woman's suffering pain in childbirth. One popular answer is that the passage speaks about Israel, the Church and Mary, a common pattern in Hebrew writing, so that some details apply more to one than the other, but the passage refers in different ways to all.

Does the Old Testament speak of Mary?

Yes, but in ways we can understand only in hindsight, when with the birth of Jesus we have the key to interpreting them. Various verses in the Old Testament have been taken as referring to Mary, although they had a meaning in their original context as well.

One verse in particular gives us a kind of divine permission to look in the Old Testament for prophecies about Mary. Isaiah declares that a virgin will conceive a son and call him Immanuel (Isaiah 7:14), and the angel who appears to Joseph in a dream quotes this verse as a prediction of the birth of Jesus (see Matthew 1:22–23). So that verse we know looks forward to Mary, which gives us reason to look for others that do.

Applying this principle, the Church has found more verses that, whatever they meant to the original writers and readers, after the Incarnation can be seen as prophecies of Mary. One good example is the very first reflection on Mary offered after the New Testament, given by Saint Justin Martyr and Saint Irenaeus in the second century.

They saw that part of God's declarations to the fallen Adam and Eve and to the serpent can be read as referring to Mary and her son. Before our first parents' exile from the garden, God tells the serpent, "I will put enmity between you and the woman, and between your seed and her seed; he shall bruise your head, and you shall bruise his heel" (Genesis 3:15). "The woman," the Fathers said, can refer to Mary, whose son bruised the serpent's head, the Second Eve whose obedience reversed the disobedience of the first Eve, just as her Son is the Second Adam whose obedience saved us from the disobedience of the first Adam (Romans 5:19).[3]

Does the New Testament use the Old Testament to speak of her?

Some of the New Testament writers, particularly Saint Luke, incorporate into their writing allusions to the Old Testament that signal to the alert reader the deeper meaning of the story they're telling. The allusions may be obscure to us, because we don't know the Scriptures as well as the original readers and hearers of the New Testament books, at least the Jewish ones (though even the gentile ones had Jewish apostles and fellow believers to explain the allusions to them).

The story of the Annunciation in Luke's Gospel offers a good example. Indeed, the presence of the angel Gabriel may be a divine allusion or reminder, since he appeared to Daniel to tell him that an anointed one would come but would also be cut down (see Daniel 9:20–27). The story begins with Gabriel's greeting to Mary, which is an allusion to the prophet Zephaniah's declaration to the people of Israel, the "daughter of Zion" (Zephaniah 3:14–17). Gabriel then tells Mary that her son will have the throne of His ancestor David, an allusion to Nathan's prophecy, delivered to David himself, that God would make a descendant of his a king and make his rule "firm forever" (2 Samuel 7:12–16, *NAB*).

When Mary asks how she can possibly have a child, Gabriel tells her that the Holy Spirit will come upon her and the Most High will "overshadow" her. This is an allusion, an unmistakable one, to the ark of the covenant in its tent, which was overshadowed by a cloud that the people of Israel saw as a sign of God's presence in the ark and with them (for an example, see Exodus 40:16–21, 34–35).

Gabriel ends his announcement, "With God nothing will be impossible" (Luke 1:37), referring to Elizabeth's conception of Saint John the Baptist, an allusion to another impossible birth, that of Isaac to Sarah, the barren wife of Abraham (see Genesis 18:14). The reader is meant to think of the man Saint Paul called "the father of us all" (Romans 4:16) and the ways in which his unshakable faith in God and God's promises were both rewarded and grew into the people of Israel, through whom God gave the world its Savior.

These allusions are just allusions, meant to expand and amplify the meaning of the story. They are not allegories, and not every detail in the original Old Testament passage applies to Mary or Jesus. Nathan's prophecy, for example, includes a

statement about correcting David's heir and the fu
Samuel 7:14), which would not apply to the Son of G

Continued allusions can be found in the story of Mary's visit
to Elizabeth, with parallels to the story of the movement of the
ark (see 2 Samuel 6:1–19). This illustrates the way the allusions
can tell us something about the story of Jesus by its contrast with
the original. When Mary arrives at her cousin's house, Elizabeth
humbly asks, "And why is this granted me, that the mother of
my Lord should come to me?" (Luke 1:43), an allusion or parallel to David's question, "How can the ark of the LORD come to
me?" (2 Samuel 6:9). Crucially, however, David cried out in
fear, having seen a man die because he accidentally touched the
ark, while Elizabeth cries out in wonder and joy. In Jesus holiness is made safe.

Can Mary be seen in the Old Testament in any other way?
Yes, by seeing images or anticipations of Mary (or "types," as
biblical scholars put it) in the Old Testament. The Church
believes that "the plan of salvation," as John Paul II explains it,
"orders the prefigurations of the Old Testament to fulfillment
in the New Covenant." These types anticipate the future reality,
while "in Mary the spiritual reality signified is already emi-
nently present."[4]

Types of Mary can be seen in Eve, Sarah, Rebekah, Rachel,
Leah, Deborah, Jochebed, Miriam, Judith, Esther, Tamar,
Rahab, Ruth and Bathsheba. Things in the Old Testament have
also been taken as types of Mary. These include the Garden of
Eden, the city of Jerusalem, Noah's ark, the ark of the covenant,

Jacob's ladder, Aaron's staff, Solomon's temple, the bridge in the Song of Songs (cited in the liturgy of her feasts, meaning that the Church accepts this image as applying to Mary) and even Gideon's fleece.

In each of these the Church has found some aspect of Mary's person and work. Most obviously, again, Mary is the New Eve, the mother of the truly living, as Eve "was the mother of all living" (Genesis 3:20), and the mother of the Son of Man as Eve was the mother of men. But this type comes with a twist that shows who Mary is by contrasting her with Eve. Mary is the New Eve who obeys the Lord and brings Jesus and redemption into the world, while the old Eve disobeyed God and thereby brought sin and death into the world. Whereas Eve disregarded God's instructions and believed the serpent when he asked, "Did God say... ?" (Genesis 3:1), Mary said, "Let it be to me according to your word" (Luke 1:38).

The ark of the covenant is another type, with Mary being the ark (or bearer) of the new covenant, as the original ark contained within itself the tablets of the Law that God had given His people as an expression and mark of the first covenant. The ark was therefore for the people of Israel a kind of Good News or gospel and a Word of God, and the child Mary carries is the Good News incarnate and the Word of God incarnate. The early Christians applied to her the psalmist's praise: "Arise, O LORD, and go to your resting place, you and the ark of your might" (Psalm 132:8). This title was one the angel Gabriel gave by allusion in the story of the Annunciation, in his declaration that she shall be overshadowed by the Most High (Luke 1:35). It is, in other words, an overtly biblical allusion that encourages us to find others.

Doesn't this kind of reading of the Old Testament find in it more than it really says?

Some biblical scholars will deny that the Old Testament can be read this way and insist that it can be read only as its original readers would have read it. They argue that it tells of the developing history and deepening knowledge of God that led up to the Incarnation but does not anticipate it so directly.

Both *Dei Verbum* and the Marian chapter in *Lumen Gentium* make clear that the Old Testament can and should be read as anticipating the New. Jesus himself gives an example of this sort of reading when he instructs the disciples as they are walking to Emmaus. "Beginning with Moses and all the prophets, he interpreted to them in all the Scriptures the things concerning himself" (Luke 24:27).

As *Dei Verbum* put it,

> God, the inspirer and author of both Testaments, wisely arranged that the New Testament be hidden in the Old and that the Old be made manifest in the New.... [T]he books of the Old Testament with all their parts, caught up into the proclamation of the Gospel, acquire and show forth their full meaning in the New Testament (see Matthew 5:17; Luke 24:27; Romans 16:25-26; 2 Corinthians 14:16) and in turn shed light on it and explain it.[5]

As *Lumen Gentium* put it in considering Mary's place in the Old Testament, the Church, reading these books with its knowledge of the later and complete revelation, sees Mary in them coming "into a gradually clearer light." The Church sees her "prophetically foreshadowed" in passages like God's declaration to the serpent, which it gives as an example.[6]

This "typological reading" does not deny or negate the original reading and the continuing value of the original reading. It simply finds that, as one might expect, the inspired writers said more than they knew they were saying.

What does Mary do in the Gospels after she bears Jesus?

Her later appearances in the Gospels are few but all significant. First, at the wedding at Cana she tells the servants to do what Jesus says, which leads to his first miracle. Some have seen in this a sign of her future intercession, as she goes to Jesus with requests from other people and He grants her requests.

Then, in the only story told of her during Jesus' public ministry, she and Jesus' "brethren" come to talk with Him. Jesus seems to put them down, asking, "Who are my mother and my brethren?" and declaring that whoever does the will of His Father is really His mother and brother (Mark 3:31–35). More about this below.

Then Mary follows Jesus, nearly alone, to the cross. There she and the Beloved Disciple accept his instruction and thereby form the first fellowship of the Church that will continue His redeeming work in the world.

Finally, she is with the apostles after the Ascension (Acts makes a point of saying that she was there). Presumably she is still with them when the Holy Spirit descends upon them a few days later, as many years before she was the first to receive the Holy Spirit, when she conceived Jesus.

Didn't Jesus declare that Mary was not important when he said that whoever does the will of His Father is really His mother?

Some anti-Marian writers (and there are such, sadly) have been quick to use this passage as evidence that after Jesus left home, His mother was no longer important in the story of His life and does not deserve the attention, much less the status, the Church has given her. (They also use Luke 11:27–28 to put her down.)

If they are right about this passage, then the later story of Mary at the cross and the inclusion of her with the apostles after the Ascension have no particular theological or devotional meaning but just record facts, presumably reflecting the care people would naturally give to the widowed mother of their leader. Indeed, if they are right about this passage, Mary's place in Jesus' conception and birth has no particular theological or devotional meaning either, and she was simply the way God got His Son into the world. (I have heard Protestant pastors say this.)

And Jesus' words are shocking, at first glance. They are not at all what you expect. But the anti-Marian reading ignores an irony planted in the story itself and certainly intended by Jesus: Mary herself is the supreme and perfect example of a human being who did and does the will of His Father. She began His life with her "Let it be to me according to your word."

Jesus was not dismissing Mary but making a point. He is not declaring her superseded by His disciples but extending the gift given to the immaculately conceived Mother of God to everyone who turns to Him and His Father. He is saying to a rather ragtag and as yet inadequate group of followers, "As she is, you can be also." He is also stressing how extraordinarily close we can be to Him, as close as His mother.

What does Saint Paul say about her?

Paul mentions Mary once, though not by name, in his Letter to the Galatians (4:4), where he refers to Jesus' being "born of woman." But do not draw any conclusions from his relative silence: Paul was an evangelist and pastor, and in his letters that we have he was concerned to spell out the central Christian message and to guide the churches he founded. Mary was not the subject he was writing about.

Even so, the Galatians passage says that Mary was part of God's plan from the beginning of time. It also suggests her importance as a kind of bridge connecting the old covenant and the new. Through her Jesus was truly and fully a man like all of us, "born under the law," as well as the Son of God, and therefore able to bring His adopted brothers to His Father. As the expression goes, this is not nothing.

Why doesn't Mary appear more often in the Bible?

This relative absence does seem like a problem to someone who loves both the Scriptures as God's Word and Mary as Jesus' mother. We expect to hear about her a lot more, given how big a place she has in the Church's life.

One simple answer is that the writers, speaking under the inspiration of the Holy Spirit, were writing for particular purposes, and Scripture only deals with any subject enough to serve the purposes for which God gave it to us. As John Paul II noted, Mary may not be mentioned more often because "what is necessary for our saving knowledge was entrusted to the word of those 'chosen by God as witnesses' (Acts 10:41), that is, the Apostles," who wrote what they needed for their purposes.[7]

Matthew and Luke supply details about Jesus' birth and early life—presumably both to fill out the story and establish that Jesus really is man as well as God. The Gospels go on to tell us what Jesus said and did, Acts describes how the early Church grew, and the epistles address the needs of the people and churches to which they were written. The New Testament writers did not need to say more about Mary than they did. They say as much as God has given them to say.

Another answer biblical scholars give is that where and how Mary is mentioned is more important than how often, and the structures of the Gospels give us some idea of her importance in the life of Jesus and of the early Church. John's Gospel only mentions her twice, for example, but the story of the wedding at Cana says more than it would seem to say at first reading. It takes place "on the third day," which points the reader to the Resurrection on the third day, as does Jesus' mentioning his "hour" that has not yet come and His calling His mother "woman," which He will do again at the cross.

As *Behold Your Mother* understands the Cana passage, it presents Mary in two ways that tell us more than it seems to about her and her place in God's work of salvation. On the one side she "is the figure of the synagogue, Daughter of Zion of old, still making use of the imperfect means of the past, the water in the stone jars." But on the other, when she tells the waiters to do what Jesus tells them to do, "she becomes the figure of the new

People of God" and "figure of the Church, Bride of Christ." This simple story shows her as the bridge between the Testaments, the deep implications of which theologians can draw out.[8]

Does the Church have any more knowledge of Mary than this?
The relative absence of Mary's mention in Scripture does not leave us without more information. God provided the generations to come not only with a Scripture but with a Church. This Church has a memory, an oral tradition reliably passed on from one generation to the next. It is expressed in her liturgy, the writings of her earliest saints and theologians, her calendar, her piety, her devotion, her doctrinal development and the dogmatic decisions of her popes, bishops and councils.

It is the "living tradition" described by the bishops at the Second Vatican Council in the Dogmatic Constitution on Divine Revelation, *Dei Verbum*. "It is not from sacred Scripture alone that the Church draws her certainty about everything which has been revealed," it says. This Sacred Tradition is "to be accepted and venerated with the same sense of loyalty and reverence" as Scripture. With Scripture it "flow[s] from the same divine wellspring" and forms "one sacred deposit of the word of God, committed to the Church."[9] Sacred Tradition carries what the Church knows and teaches about Mary that is not conveyed, or conveyed overtly, in the Sacred Scriptures.

Don't Catholics draw from the New Testament stories about Mary more than they really say?
Catholics who have reflected on the Bible have drawn many lessons and insights from its stories about Mary. These might be

divided into certain or almost certain, probable, very possible, possible, a stretch and far-fetched. (Of course, a lesson might be far-fetched—that is, might find in Scripture what it does not really say—and still be true.)

Devotion to the Mother of our Lord does tempt some Catholics, including homilists, to find in the biblical text more than it actually says and to insist on certainty in matters that do not allow it. We must know the biblical text well and evaluate any particular claims in the light of what we know about Mary through the biblical stories and the Church's teaching.

The interpretation given above of Jesus' question "Who are my mother and my brethren?" seems to me an example of a certain or almost certain reading. The story of the wedding at Cana gives an example of what seem to me to be possible and very possible readings. Some have seen in Mary's telling Jesus that the hosts had run out of wine, and her confidently telling the servants to do what Jesus told them, evidence that Jesus performed a lot of miracles at home, so that Mary naturally assumed that he would perform one here. This is a possible reading. Jesus' response to her is often used as an argument for praying to Mary to ask Jesus for help on our behalf. The hosts or the servants went to Mary, it is assumed, and she went to Jesus with their request, and He granted it. This is a very possible reading.

Neither reading is impossible or even unlikely, by any means, but neither is clearly given in the text. They are both speculation, not exegesis.

Does the Church teach anything about Mary that can't be found in the Bible?

Yes, if by "can't be found" you mean "is not stated explicitly," in the sense that someone with no knowledge of Christianity who had only the Bible for information would not think of it. But, no, if you mean something utterly separate from the biblical revelation.

The Catholic reading of Scripture depends on the belief that Scripture is not a haphazard collection of historical documents, not even a haphazard collection of *inspired* historical documents, but that it has a unity that expresses God's intention—not the obvious structural unity of a book of mathematical theorems but the unity of an artist's vision. Passages from different books can illuminate each other because each reflects some aspect of a single message or story ultimately told by a single storyteller. This single intention includes truths passed on by speech and not in writing.

Scripture and Tradition relate to each other subtly, like parts of a vision. The world's bishops were careful, in explaining the Church's teaching in *Dei Verbum*, to say that the apostles "by their oral preaching, by example, and by observances handed on what they had received from the lips of Christ, from living with Him, and from what He did, or what they had learned through the prompting of the Holy Spirit," as well as by writing the Scriptures. Both sources of truth, "flowing from the same divine wellspring, in a certain way merge into a unity and tend toward the same end."[10]

Thus some things the Church teaches can only be found in

the Bible by looking backward from what the Church knows in other ways.

What major teachings are seen in the Bible by looking backward?

The perpetual virginity of Mary and the Immaculate Conception are not found overtly in Scripture, but knowing them to be true, the reader can find traces and hints in Scripture. They might even be called "echoes" of a truth from the future the inspired writer saw. They are biblical doctrines, but not overtly biblical doctrines.

Mary's sinlessness, for example, a belief that appears in the sources we have early in the Church's history—and which we assume goes back to the beginning of the Church—can be seen to be assumed in Gabriel's "Hail, full of grace" (Luke 1:28). It is part of what the angel meant, though the reader who has only the words before him would probably not see that. If she was full of grace, she could not be sinful. There would not be any room for sin, grace having filled up the space, if I may put it that way.

The dogma of the Immaculate Conception, the more precise form in which that early belief came to be stated, can also be seen to be required by the story of "the woman," taken to mean Mary, whose son would crush the serpent's head (see Genesis 3:15). If she suffered even for a moment from the inherited stain of sin—if she were subject to original sin, in other words—she would not have had that "perpetual enmity" with the serpent of which the passage speaks. Once the answer is understood, the deeper meaning of the angel's greeting (and Elizabeth's) becomes clearer.

The Assumption of Mary is a more difficult matter, from this point of view, because the traces and hints in Scripture are not as easily found. In *Munificentissimus Deus* Pius XII says only that the dogma "is in wonderful accord with those divine truths given us in Holy Scripture," and while he quotes a great many Fathers and theologians thereafter, they argue mainly from tradition or from a sense of what is fitting for Mary given what we know of her. In introducing their arguments, in fact, Pius remarks on those who "have been rather free in their use of events and expressions taken from Sacred Scripture to explain their belief in the Assumption."[11]

Nevertheless, he sees the teaching as implicit in Mary as the New Eve. Because she "is most intimately associated" with Jesus, the New Adam, in the "struggle against the infernal foe," their shared struggle "should be brought to a close by the glorification of her virginal body, for the same apostle [Paul] says: 'When this mortal thing hath put on immortality, then shall come to pass the saying that is written: Death is swallowed up in victory' [1 Corinthians 15:54]."[12] Nevertheless, here the Church would seem to have seen the truth without being able to argue for it fully, a matter addressed in the next chapter.

Where we will also address this question of Scripture, Tradition and dogma from a different angle. There is more to be said.

CHAPTER THREE

MARY IN CATHOLIC DOCTRINE

The Church often declares what she sees before she can completely explain and defend what she has said—not that we can ever completely explain and defend the mysteries, coming as they do from God. This is especially true of her Marian doctrines. Putting her knowledge into more and more precise words is not like working out a mathematical proof from premises; it's more like trying to understand something in the heavens long seen in telescopes but only coming into focus as instruments improve and understanding of astronomy grows.

I mention this to explain why some Marian teaching, not least the papal declarations of the Immaculate Conception and the Assumption, strike some readers as unsatisfying. They expect the kind of conclusive, final argument you get in geometry class, and they find instead an argument that is to some extent a collection of sources and a description of the meaning. It is more like a trial lawyer's list of witnesses and exhibits and less like his final summation.

As a modern philosopher said about mere human knowledge, we know more than we can say. We know much about our parents that we cannot prove by argument, because we know them. We know that Dad will hate a surprise birthday party, just because we know him, when someone who does not know him as well may argue convincingly that he'll love it because he is always up for something new. We know Dad, from a vast amount of experience and observation, though we don't know exactly what we know.

In the same way, our belief in the Church's Marian teaching is perfectly rational but not always perfectly arguable. That explains why much apologetic argument can seem thin or stretched: It is addressed to people who do not accept the basic Catholic claim that knowledge of such realities has been passed down to us through the Church. These people do not know what we know, and thus they can't see what we see.

But this is not something to worry about. Our first calling is to believe and adore and, believing and adoring, to try to understand and only then, understanding as well as we can, to try to explain and share.

What is Mariology?

Mariology is the theological study of Mary, the Mother of God. As there are systematic theologians, Christologists, ecclesiologists and biblical scholars, so there are Mariologists. The study can be divided into two parts, one reflecting on Mary's work and mission as the Mother of God, the other on what are called her "privileges" or "prerogatives," like the Immaculate Conception and the Assumption.

Mariology is not an independent discipline, but one pursued in coordination with the other branches of theology. We don't study it to learn more about Mary alone but to learn more about her place in God's work. Mariology depends upon the biblical scholar to use the tools of his discipline to understand a text, but it offers the biblical scholar insights into Mary that may help him understand the text more deeply.

Mariology begins with the data. We don't study it to create, by speculation and imagination, more teachings about Mary, but rather to understand more deeply and express more clearly what the Church has already seen about her.

How did the teaching on Mary develop in the early Church?

The Church began as a small, evangelistic community, often persecuted. Her main need, an almost overwhelmingly difficult need, was to proclaim the Christ. To the extent this small but steadily growing group had the people and the time for theology, their energy had to be directed to explaining who Jesus is, especially why He is the only Savior in a world that was happy to add Him to its list of gods and expected Christians to return the favor, and got annoyed when they didn't.

As the Church grew, and began to face new challenges and have more members gifted to think theologically with the freedom to do so, she began to reflect more on other matters. These included the place of Jesus' mother in the Good News Christians were proclaiming and living.

The early Church was a bit like a class for people who want to enter the Church but don't know much about religion or

Christianity at all, people who have truly seen the Lord in His Church without quite knowing what they've seen. In teaching them the faith, we begin with Jesus and treat the other matters as they radiate from Him. These people have all sorts of odd ideas about Jesus that need to be corrected—that He was just a really wise man, for example, or that He achieved godhood by being so amazingly good—and we will tell them about Scripture or the Church or Mary only as that knowledge helps them understand Jesus. Once they know clearly who Jesus is, they will want and need to learn more about these other parts of the story. When they can say the Nicene Creed with full agreement, they will want to know why the Virgin Mary it proclaims was immaculately conceived and assumed into Heaven, and why that matters.

Very broadly speaking, the Church's thinking about Mary, from the end of the biblical period through the middle of the fifth century and the General Council of Chalcedon, was Christological, meaning that it was mainly concerned to speak of Mary in speaking more precisely of Christ. But beginning in the third century and continuing to the end of the sixth, the Church's thinking about Mary became more ecclesiological, meaning that it was more and more concerned with her place in the Church and her continuing life. After that the Church continued to refine her understanding of Mary in relation to Christ and the Church's life but also to explore more deeply what we now think of as Marian devotion.

What did the earlier Church Fathers say about Mary?

Answering this question requires summarizing very briefly a long and complex development. (The Fathers give us much meat in this as in other matters, making them worth reading extensively and closely. This very short summary will inevitably make them look as if they only gave us skim milk. It's like describing Michelangelo's *David* by saying, "He did the human figure well.") The pattern was described in the previous question, but more specifically:

The first Fathers, the group of the second century usually called the "Apostolic Fathers," began by stressing that Jesus was born of Mary and insisting that she was a virgin, because they were mainly concerned to tell and to explain the story of Jesus as the world's Savior. The first reference we have to Mary after the New Testament comes from Saint Ignatius, about AD 110, only a few decades after the last book of the New Testament was written. In his letters to the Ephesians and the Trallians, Ignatius asserts that Jesus really was a man, born of Mary, who was a virgin. Later in the century Saint Justin Martyr and Saint Irenaeus both describe Mary in relation to Eve, Irenaeus declaring that as man fell into death by a virgin, so he was saved by a virgin.

The Fathers of the third and especially the fourth century—the century when the Church was made legal and held her first general council—began to reflect more deeply on Mary as the Mother of God. This was part of a deepening understanding of who Jesus is, especially in response to various theories (heresies, in a word) recognized as being dangerously wrong. Their arguments over Mary began in arguments over Christ.

For example, Christians had been calling Mary *Theotokos*— meaning "God bearer" in Greek, or more accurately "the one who gave birth to God"—for some time.[1] The Fathers began to assert it more strenuously in response to Nestorius, a patriarch of Constantinople, who would call her only *Christotokos*, meaning "Christ bearer." He had good reasons, among them that the title *Theotokos* might diminish Jesus' humanity, but other Fathers saw that his solution implied that there were two persons in Christ, not one. Mary would seem to be the mother of the human person, while the divine person would be superimposed on Him. If Nestorius's title were accepted, eventually Jesus would not be known as truly God and truly man.

Something had to be done. The Third General Council, held in Ephesus in 431, definitively declared Mary the *Theotokos* and condemned Nestorius and his view. His error was thought so serious that he was deprived of his see and confined under guard in monasteries for the rest of his life.

The orthodox theologians began to offer an extensive and subtle description of exactly how Mary's motherhood is related to both the human and divine natures of Christ and how these natures relate to each other. Scholars now debate the details of the argument, including whether Nestorius really believed what others thought he believed. In any case the debate helped the Church make her understanding of Mary more exact, but—and this is crucial—in order to protect and preserve her understanding of Jesus.

What did the later Church Fathers say about Mary?
The Fathers soon began to think of Mary ecclesiologically. They began to reflect on her as a type, or image, of the Church. Saint Ambrose, for example, said that "the role of the church, like that

of Mary, is to conceive by the Spirit and to bring new children into the world."[2] About this time the Fathers began to use the biblical idea of the Church as a body and to reflect that as Mary gave Jesus His body, so she in some sense was the mother of the body of Christ and the Mother of the Church.

The Fathers in this period also began to discuss Mary's perpetual virginity and to speak of her not just as "the virgin" but as "ever virgin." Christians began to call her "all holy" and to assert that she had not sinned. In the fifth century they also began to reflect on the end of her life and assert that she was assumed into Heaven. (These beliefs go back to the beginning, we assume.)

Has Marian doctrine grown since the Fathers? Does the Church today say more about her than did the Church of the first centuries?

Yes, sort of, but mainly no.

Yes, because the Church has come to a developed and refined understanding of matters like her Immaculate Conception, which was argued over fiercely into the late Middle Ages. No, because what the Church says today is only developed and refined, not expanded. A modern theologian could sit down with a third-century Father and explain the development of the doctrine of the Immaculate Conception, and half an hour later the Father would say that this is indeed what he and his peers believed.

The reader of the Fathers will be struck by how strong were their statements about Mary—stronger, indeed, than the more reticent mode of the last two centuries. In the first chapter we saw a flat assertion by Saint John Chrysostom matched by a more guarded statement of the same idea by Pope John Paul II.

In the Fathers we find definitive statements like Saint Irenaeus's "[A]s the human race fell into bondage to death by means of a virgin, so is it rescued by a virgin; virginal disobedience having been balanced in the opposite scale by virginal obedience," and Saint Ephrem's "Only you [Jesus] and your Mother are more beautiful than everything. For on you, O Lord, there is no mark; neither is there any stain in your Mother."[3] Saint Epiphanius declared, "Mary, the holy Virgin, is truly great before God and men. For how shall we not proclaim her great, who held within her the uncontainable One, whom neither heaven nor earth can contain?"[4]

It is hard to think of a modern statement stronger about Mary than these. It is useful to know that Epiphanius also declared: "Mary should be honored, but only God should be worshipped."[5]

What are the major Marian doctrines?

In the order they happened in Mary's life: her Immaculate Conception, her becoming the Mother of God, her perpetual virginity and her Assumption. They are all ancient beliefs, although the doctrinal formulation of the first was a matter of intense debate well into the Middle Ages. The Immaculate Conception and the Assumption have only been made dogma in the last two centuries.

Isn't it a little late in Church history to be declaring new dogmas about Mary? After all, the Creed we say at Mass was settled way back in the fifth century.

No, not at all. Many of us assume that the period of the Fathers ran for five or six or seven centuries and then stopped, and that all the councils and popes thereafter just developed or explained doctrines that had been articulated and settled by then. That is not a Catholic conception of Church history, which recognizes that the Church has, or indeed is, a living tradition, and that she has a magisterium that allows secure growth in our knowledge of the truth. The Church imposes no time limit on what God may teach her.

As the writer Ronald Knox noted, for all we know we are still living in the age of the Fathers. Catholics in the future may look at the declaration of the Assumption in 1950 the way we look at the Council of Chalcedon in 451, as the result of a necessarily time-consuming growth in understanding and articulation, which was finally declared when the Church had a chance and a reason to declare it. They may see the Church's needing almost two thousand years to state formally her belief in Mary's assumption into Heaven as no odder than her needing four-hundred-some years to come to the definition of Christ given in the Chalcedonian definition. They may see Saint Thomas's arguing against the Immaculate Conception in the fourteenth century as no more an argument against it than Origen's arguing in the second century for universalism. These things take time.

The fundamental matter for the Catholic is not the question "When did the Church say this?" but the belief that the Church has been given authority to teach in the name of Jesus, and when, under the guidance of the Spirit, she comes to a clearer understanding of what God has revealed in Christ, she teaches it. Such matters are declared at "the moment appointed in the plan of divine providence," as Pius XII wrote about his declaration of the Assumption.[6]

What does the Church think she is doing when she declares dogmas about Mary like the Immaculate Conception and the Assumption?

Simply declaring a truth she has been given to declare. As Pope Pius XII said in *Munificentissimus Deus*, the Church's teaching authority has been entrusted (Pius's word) with a commission: "that of preserving the revealed truths pure and entire throughout every age, in such a way that it presents them undefiled, adding nothing to them and taking nothing away from them."[7] The authority is a witness, not an inventor; it is a reporter, not a novelist.

This explains the care with which Pius IX and Pius XII proceeded before making any statements on the Immaculate Conception and the Assumption, and why they consulted with so many people, not just the cardinals and the bishops. In his encyclical letter *Ubi Primum*, sent to the world's bishops in 1849, Pope Saint Pius IX asked for prayers

> that the most merciful Father of all knowledge will deign to enlighten Us with the heavenly light of His Holy Spirit, so that in a matter of such moment We may proceed to do what will redound to the greater glory of His Holy Name, to the

honor of the most Blessed Virgin, and to the profit of the Church Militant.[8]

He was clearly convinced of the truth of the doctrine, but he would not proclaim it before God showed him it was time to do so.

This understanding of the Church as a witness also explains why the encyclicals these popes issued are so carefully worded and so limited in what they declare. We may expect something like a Renaissance painting with hundreds of characters and details in it, but we find something closer to a simple pen-and-ink drawing.

The Fathers, especially the Fathers of the early councils, regarded their work in the same way. They didn't declare Mary the Mother of God because they thought it a good thing to say but because they thought it expressed the truth about her and her son that they had received. They spoke when events forced them to think the matter through and say more precisely what some Christians were already saying, almost always because some others were saying things that weren't true. The later Church has had the blessing of being able to develop her teaching on Mary over time, without having to respond to threats and crises.

What does the official declaration of the doctrine of the Immaculate Conception say?

Issued by Pope Pius IX in the Apostolic Constitution *Ineffabilis Deus* (meaning "God ineffable") on December 8, 1854, the definition declares that

the doctrine which holds that the most Blessed Virgin Mary, in the first instance of her conception, by a singular grace and privilege granted by Almighty God, in view of the merits of Jesus Christ, the Savior of the human race, was preserved free from all stain of original sin, is a doctrine revealed by God and therefore to be believed firmly and constantly by all the faithful.[9]

The Immaculate Conception is called a "privilege" because it is an exception to the law and one that God has given no other creature.

The word *immaculate* doesn't simply mean "perfect." It comes from the Latin words for "not" and "to stain." The doctrine emphasizes Mary's freedom from moral corruption, that is, not what she is in herself but what she is by the grace of God. Theologians have said that this freedom includes the freedom from disordered and unruly desires, what moral theologians call "concupiscence," the kind of feelings that corrupt us even when we do not consciously intend to do wrong. God, in other words, freed Mary not only from original sin but from the possibility of sliding into sin. He ensured that her desires and feelings were always rightly ordered.

How important did Pius IX think this doctrine?

Very—indeed ultimately. He declared that any Catholic who rejects it is "condemned by his own judgment." The dissenter should know "that he has suffered shipwreck in the faith; that he has separated from the unity of the Church; and that, furthermore, by his own action he incurs the penalties established by law if he should dare to express in words or writing or by any other outward means the errors he thinks in his heart."[10]

How this applies to Protestants is a question above my pay grade, but the Second Vatican Council's Decree on Ecumenism, *Unitatis Redintegratio*, suggests that their ignorance of the truth may spare them guilt.[11] Still, to deny the doctrine and the ancient tradition it focuses is to deny something about Mary that the Church has long known.

How did Pius IX argue for the doctrine?

As I said in the beginning of the chapter, it is probably better to say that he explained it than that he argued for it. In a declaration like this, the Holy Father is not trying to convince others but declaring a truth that all Catholics must believe. But as a pastor, conscious of the human need and desire for reasons, he gives a basic explanation.

In outline: Pius begins by declaring that God foresaw Adam's sin and decreed the incarnation of His Son so that man would not die, and that he prepared a mother for His Son. He then adds that "far above all the angels and all the saints so wondrously did God endow her with the abundance of all heavenly gifts poured from the treasury of his divinity that this mother, ever absolutely free of all stain of sin, all fair and perfect, would possess that fullness of holy innocence and sanctity than which, under God, one cannot even imagine anything greater, and which, outside of God, no mind can succeed in comprehending fully."

He then explains the doctrine in terms of the fitness that the Son of God should have such a mother, the Church's liturgical practice in celebrating the Feast of the Immaculate Conception, and the teaching and practice of previous popes, which he reviews at some length. He notes the agreement of religious orders, eminent theologians and bishops, the "intimation" of the Council of Trent and the testimony "of venerable antiquity, of both the Eastern and the Western Church." He then summarizes the biblical arguments offered by "the Fathers and writers of the Church" and their "explicit affirmation" of the doctrine.[12]

How did the pope decide to make this official definition?

Even with all the evidence he presented in *Ineffabilis Deus*, Pius IX proceeded "with great prudence." In addition to continuing his own fervent prayers, he established a congregation of cardinals and learned priests to study the matter, and he asked all the world's bishops what they thought about defining the doctrine and what they observed as "the piety and devotion of their faithful." Having received a positive response from the cardinals, the theologians and the bishops, and through the bishops their people, he then called a consistory (a meeting of the cardinals) to discuss it. The cardinals asked him to promulgate the doctrine.

How much support is there for this doctrine in the Church's tradition?

As Pope Pius IX stated, a great deal. Though defining the dogma took nineteen centuries, this understanding of Mary had been percolating in and shaping the Church's thinking since the first centuries of her life. Remember Saint Ephrem's description of Jesus and Mary as "more beautiful than everything. For on You, O Lord, there is no mark, neither is there any stain in Your Mother."[13] All the dogma does is put this teaching in a more precise form.

What is the doctrine of the perpetual virginity?

The belief that Mary remained a virgin throughout her whole life. The belief is ancient and nearly universal, with only a couple of dissenters, the most famous being the third-century Father Tertullian, who went off the rails in other ways as well. The title "ever virgin" was given to Mary by the Fifth General Council, held in Constantinople in 553. It declared her "always a virgin" and "the holy, glorious, and ever-virgin Mary, the Mother of God."[14] It did so in the course of defending an exact and orthodox understanding of Christ.

The perpetual virginity includes three separate stages: first, that Mary conceived Jesus of the Holy Spirit and not of a man (what we think of as the virgin birth but is more accurately called the virginal conception); second, that she remained a virgin when giving birth to Christ (sometimes called the "virginal parturition"); and third, that she remained a virgin after Jesus was born. As the fourth-century Father Saint Augustine put it, in a saying that became common, "A virgin conceived, a virgin bore, and after the birth was a virgin still."[15]

Almost all Christians until very recently have agreed with this, though there was some argument in the early Church about the second stage. Most of the founders of Protestantism believed in it firmly. One of the more radical, the Swiss reformer Zwingli, declared late in his life, "I believe with all my heart according to the word of holy gospel that this pure virgin bore for us the Son of God and that she remained, in the birth and after it, a pure and unsullied virgin, for eternity."[16] Luther declared late in his life that "Mary remained a virgin. For after she had perceived that she was the mother of the Son of God, she didn't think she should become the mother of a human child."[17] The partial exception is Calvin, who refused to say whether Mary remained a virgin but criticized as "a contentious trouble-maker" anyone who argued that she had not.[18]

Today almost all Christians still believe in the first stage, but only Catholics and Orthodox still hold the second and third. Protestants speak little of these last two, even in their church histories.[19]

The first and third stages we looked at in the first chapter. The second is the least mentioned and the least understood. It holds that Mary kept her physical integrity (an intact hymen) during birth. The Fathers were much less squeamish about these things than we are, and Saint Ambrose declared somewhat graphically, "When He [Jesus] was born from His mother's womb, He yet preserved the fence of her chastity and the inviolate seal of her virginity."[20] Giving birth to Christ while remaining a virgin was as much a miracle as His miraculous conception itself—but also no more a miracle.

This belief in the virgin parturition appears early. Saint Ambrose, Saint Jerome and Saint Augustine argued for it using events from Jesus' life like His emerging from the sealed tomb[21] and His passing through closed doors after His Resurrection, and from analogies like light passing through glass and a human thought going out from the mind. Ambrose offered a biblical argument as well, writing that "Holy Mary is the gate of which it is written: 'The Lord will pass through it, and it will be shut' [Ezekiel

44:2], after birth, for as a virgin she conceived and gave birth."[22]

The virginal parturition is one of those truths the Church has seen but not developed. Most of us can see the point of the first and third stages but not so easily the meaning of this one, and even the Fathers who defended it did not say much to explain it. It may safely be said, at the least, that it is fitting that the Virgin Mother of God should remain a virgin in all aspects.

What does the official declaration of the doctrine of the Assumption say?

Issued by Pope Pius XII in the Apostolic Constitution *Munificentissimus Deus* on November 1, 1950, the definition declares that "the Immaculate Mother of God, the ever Virgin Mary, having completed the course of her earthly life, was assumed body and soul into heavenly glory."[23]

How important did Pius XII think this doctrine?

Very, and indeed ultimately. Pius XII followed the definition with a slightly different warning than Pius IX's warning about the Immaculate Conception, but one no less forceful. "It is forbidden to any man," he declared, "to change this, our declaration, pronouncement, and definition or, by rash attempt, to oppose and counter it. If any man should presume to make such an attempt, let him know that he will incur the wrath of Almighty God and of the Blessed Apostles Peter and Paul."[24]

The qualification given in answer to this question when asked about the Immaculate Conception applies: that is, ignorance of the truth may alleviate guilt.

How did Pius XII argue for the doctrine of the Assumption?

Pius XII begins by describing the desire of the faithful for the doctrine to be defined and explaining how it follows from the doctrine of the Immaculate Conception: by this "entirely unique privilege" Mary "was not subject to the law of remaining in the corruption of the grave, and she did not have to wait until the end of time for the redemption of her body." The pope then describes the growing desire of the faithful for the dogma and the nearly unanimous agreement of the world's bishops, declaring that "from the universal agreement of the Church's ordinary teaching authority we have a certain and firm proof" of Mary's assumption.

Only after this declaration does Pius XII turn to the arguments. He appeals to "various testimonies, indications and signs of this common belief of the Church [that] are evident from remote times down through the course of the centuries." These include the belief of the early Christians; the naming of churches after the Assumption; the liturgical observances of Mary's death; the homilies of the Fathers and the great theologians; the arguments of medieval theologians, like Saint Thomas Aquinas and Saint Anthony of Padua; the fact that the Assumption "is in wonderful accord with those divine truths given us in Holy Scripture"; and the arguments of later theologians, like Saint Robert Bellarmine and Saint Francis de Sales. He then offers one argument of his own, from Mary as the New Eve.[25]

He summarizes:

Hence the revered Mother of God, from all eternity joined in a hidden way with Jesus Christ in one and the same decree of predestination, immaculate in her conception, a most perfect virgin in her divine motherhood, the noble associate of the divine Redeemer who has won a complete triumph over sin and its consequences, finally obtained, as the supreme culmination of her privileges, that she should be preserved free from the corruption of the tomb and that, like her own Son, having overcome death, she might be taken up body and soul to the glory of heaven where, as Queen, she sits in splendor at the right hand of her Son, the immortal King of the Ages.[26]

How did the pope decide to make an official definition?

While many people in the Church asked him to define the doctrine officially, Pius XII was careful to ask for theological inquiry first. He also asked the world's bishops to give him their views and the views of their people, which proved almost unanimous.

How does the Church come to doctrines like the Immaculate Conception and the Assumption that aren't explicitly given in Scripture?

We looked at one answer, from the point of view of the Scriptures, at the end of the last chapter. A short answer, from the point of view of doctrine, is that dogmas like the Immaculate Conception and the Assumption are "truth[s] revealed by God and contained in that divine deposit which Christ has delivered to his Spouse," as Pius XII said in *Munificentissimus Deus*.[27] The "divine deposit" includes those things "to be believed which are contained in the word of God as found in Scripture and tradition, and which are proposed by the Church as matters to be believed as divinely revealed, whether by her solemn judgment or in her ordinary and universal magisterium," in the words of the First Vatican Council's *Dogmatic Constitution on the Church of Christ*.[28]

The Church not only guards this deposit but knows what it contains. The better question to ask, in other words, is not "Is this in Scripture?" but "Is this in the divine deposit of truth given to the Church?" *Dei Verbum*—readers interested in this question should read it closely—summarizes its careful discussion of this matter this way: "[S]acred tradition, Sacred Scripture, and the teaching authority of the Church, in accord with God's most wise design, are so linked and joined together that one cannot stand without the others," and they work "all together and each in its own way under the action of the one Holy Spirit."[29]

We find a parallel in the development of the Church's understanding of Jesus. The heretics could make plausible arguments, using Scripture, for their views, but the bishops gathered at the First Council of Nicea saw the real teaching of Scripture on who Jesus is, even though they had to invent a term not found in the Bible, *homoousios*, to define it exactly. They had not only the words of Scripture but their real meaning. There is no more to object to in the developed understanding of the Immaculate Conception, declared by Pope Pius IX in 1854, than there is to object to in the developed understanding of the nature of Christ, declared in 325 by the Council of Nicea.

In *Ineffabilis Deus* Pius IX gives us a good short statement of the Church's work in these matters:

For the Church of Christ, watchful guardian that she is, and defender of the dogmas deposited with her, never changes anything, never diminishes anything, never adds anything to them; but with all diligence she treats the ancient documents faithfully and wisely; if they really are of ancient origin and if the faith of the Fathers has transmitted them, she strives to investigate and explain them in such a way that the ancient dogmas of heavenly doctrine will be made evident and clear, but will retain their full, integral, and proper nature, and will grow only within their own genus—that is, within the same dogma, in the same sense and the same meaning.[30]

One final point: Scriptural silence is not by itself any evidence that a doctrine is either untrue or a matter of opinion. As we discussed in the first chapter, the biblical writers were writing for particular purposes, which did not include sharing their entire knowledge of Mary. There is no reason for any of the New Testament writers to bring up the perpetual virginity of Mary, her assumption or the purity eventually articulated as the Immaculate Conception, and indeed they may have assumed their readers knew about it anyway.

What did the Protestant reformers say about Mary?

Perhaps surprisingly, Catholics and the new dissenters at the time of the Reformation did not at first argue much about the nature and work of Mary, though the Reformers' rejection of distinctively Catholic belief and practice increased as their separation from the Church hardened.

Although his views are, as a Lutheran pastor said to me, "a moving target," Martin Luther did not at first reject the Church's teaching on Mary and did not treat it as the crucial difference his theological descendents would do. The first of the major Protestant reformers, at least for some time after his break with the Church, he believed in the Immaculate Conception and the Assumption and could write of Mary with honor.

Hueldrich Zwingli, a contemporary of Luther and one of the more radical of the major reformers, had a very high view of Mary. Another of the more radical reformers, Heinrich Bullinger, spoke of Mary as the greatest of the saints.

John Calvin, the second of the great reformers (the Presbyterian Church descends from him) and one who rejected much more of Catholic doctrine and devotion than did Luther, was more dismissive of Marian teaching. He was particularly eager to reject any mediatorial role for Mary, believing that this denied Christ's unique place and work.

The English, reformers almost unanimously held Mary's perpetual virginity and her sinlessness. They eliminated her from the Church calendar and the liturgy, however, and their *Articles of Religion*, the Church of England's basic statement of belief, mention her only in passing, saying that Jesus "took Man's nature in the womb of the blessed Virgin, of her substance."[31]

In summary, the first reformers "wanted to give honor to Mary," argues one of the leading evangelicals of today, Timothy George, an executive editor of the major evangelical magazine *Christianity Today*.

They wanted to remind the church that she was to be called *blessed* in every generation. They honored her as the vehicle of God's grace in giving Jesus to the world and an example of justification by faith alone, because she believed so purely in the gospel. I think we need to go back and reclaim something of the Reformer's more positive view of Mary, insofar as it really is biblical. It really is part of our own Protestant heritage.[32]

I think this is the optimistic reading of the reformers, but in any case, that "insofar as it is really biblical" suggests the central difference between Catholics and Protestants on this topic. As the fathers of the Second Vatican Council recognized, there are "weighty differences" between the Catholic Church and what they call the "separated churches and ecclesial communities in the West."

These are "not only of a historical, sociological, psychological and cultural character, but especially [of the] interpretation of revealed truth," and they include Mary's role in God's work of salvation. The Protestants "think differently from us—different ones in different ways—about the relationship between the scriptures and the Church. For in the Church, according to Catholic belief, its authentic teaching office has a special place in expanding and preaching the written Word of God."[33]

What beliefs do modern Protestants share with us?

Modern Protestants differ a lot from each other, but by and large they believe in the virginal conception (it is part of the official teaching of all the mainline churches, though their modernist wings reject it) but deny that she remained a virgin during birth and after, as well as the Immaculate Conception and the

Assumption. Some who don't necessarily object theologically to either of the last two do object to their being made dogmas, because they deny that the Church has the authority to do that.

Most believe that Mary had more children after Jesus and that her role in the salvation of man was finished when Jesus left home, since the stories of her during His public ministry seem to be negative, and the New Testament does not mention her after the beginning of Acts. Most do not believe that the woman described in Revelation 12 is Mary. If she is to be remembered today, she is to be remembered only as one example of faithfulness, though a great one.

Some in the Anglican and Lutheran churches believe almost all the Catholic doctrines but generally say that these are optional beliefs, not dogmas that must be believed. In a few "high" Anglican and Lutheran churches, the Hail Mary is said during the prayers of the people, and the *Angelus* is said at noon.

There is a small movement among both evangelical and mainline Protestants to give more attention to Mary and to recover at least a deeper respect for her. They stop well short of appealing to her—you will not find them saying the rosary, for example—and affirming Catholic teaching on the Immaculate Conception and the Assumption. But they do speak of Mary more often and with more respect than their fathers or grandfathers.

But still, many of the firmest Protestants deeply oppose the Church's Marian teaching. Reinhold Niebuhr, perhaps the most influential Protestant theologian in America in the last century, declared that the Assumption "incorporates a legend of the

Middle Ages into the official teachings of the Church, thereby placing the final capstone on the Mariolatry of the Roman Church."[34] Many of his successors are just as opposed as he was.

A mainstream Anglican group I know has published a set of articles on Mary that includes statements like this: calling Mary the Mother of God "has been the source of much confusion and error," because it "implies that she shares in Christ's Divine nature and that she existed before God. In consequence, Mary has been exalted and has become an object of worship, the creature is worshipped rather than the Creator; this is plain idolatry." (Which is kind of odd, since their church's founding documents, the sixteenth-century *Articles of Religion*, accept the first four councils, and the fourth declared Mary the Mother of God.) As you can guess, they dislike teachings like the Assumption a lot more.[35]

What beliefs do the Orthodox share with us?

Though Orthodoxy's lack of a magisterium makes sound generalizations hard to make, we can say that the Orthodox Churches agree with the Catholic Church on the motherhood of God and the perpetual virginity, and in turning to her in praise and intercession. Their liturgy is in fact much more overtly Marian than ours. They agree with us in practice on the Immaculate Conception and the Assumption, while raising various theological objections to the Catholic dogmas.[36]

Most Orthodox believe in Mary's sinlessness just as strongly as Catholics do, but they do not believe in original sin in the way Catholics do—they think it "Augustinian" and "Western"—and therefore do not accept the Immaculate Conception. As the modern Russian Orthodox theologian Sergius Bulgakov declared, "The Orthodox Church does not accept the Catholic dogma of 1854—the dogma of the Immaculate Conception of the Virgin, in the sense that she was exempt at birth from original sin. This would separate her from the human race, and she would then have been unable to transmit to her Son this true humanity. But Orthodoxy does not admit in the All-pure Virgin any individual sin, for that would be unworthy of the dignity of the Mother of God."[37] But Byzantine theologians from the ninth century on could speak of Mary as "purified" from "the beginning" or "the embryo," and in the nineteenth century many Russian and Greek theologians believed in the Immaculate Conception and even rejected the papal definition not as wrong but as "superfluous." They also object to the declaration of the Immaculate Conception as a dogma by the Catholic Church.[38] In any case, the practical difference is very small.

The Orthodox also believe in Mary's assumption into Heaven, which they celebrate under the title "Dormition," though some Orthodox churches are named after the Assumption. Their only objection to this dogma is to the authority that the pope and the Catholic Church claimed in making it a dogma, but again, the practical difference is very small. Two hymns from the Orthodox liturgy give the flavor of their belief. One says:

> In falling asleep you did not forsake the world, O *Theotokos*.
> You were translated to life, O Mother of Life,
> And by your prayers, you deliver our souls from death.

The other says,

Neither the tomb, nor death could hold the *Theotokos*,
Who is constant in prayer and our firm hope in her intercessions.
For being the Mother of Life,
She was translated to life by the One who dwelt in her virginal womb.[39]

What importance do the Marian dogmas have in ecumenical relations?

The Orthodox object to the dogmas of the Immaculate Conception and the Assumption as exercises of a papal authority they do not recognize. If this more fundamental question were settled, the Marian dogmas, as well as the liturgical and devotional expressions of Marian piety, could become a clear point of unity. Even the Immaculate Conception might be understood by the Orthodox—despite their objections—as a Western expression of a truth about Mary that both Catholics and Orthodox recognize (and no one else does).

But with our Protestant friends the Marian dogmas have been, and still are, very divisive matters. Many Protestants, including the most faithful to their tradition and the most theologically serious, object to them strongly. Karl Barth, perhaps the most important and most influential Protestant theologian of the last century, thought that the Church's Marian teaching reduced or removed the need for grace. He is by no means alone in thinking that what Catholics say of Mary makes man much more than he is.

And our Protestant friends are not wrong in thinking these things important. The Marian doctrines are part of a whole intricate system of doctrine, so that if one part is got wrong the rest will be wrong as well. For one thing, these doctrines raise the question of the authority of the Church. How does the Catholic Church justify making belief in the Assumption a dogma without an overt statement of its truth in the Bible?

And for another, these doctrines raise the question of how man is saved. As *Behold Your Mother* puts it, they present the divisive problem of "what can man do under the power of grace?" The statement goes on: "What the Church has said about the effects of redemption in Mary, she has affirmed in other ways and at other times of us all. The Immaculate Conception and the Assumption...are basically affirmations about the nature of human salvation."[40] Our Protestant friends understandably object to our understanding of Mary, given what they think about salvation.

CHAPTER FOUR

THE FEASTS OF MARY

While many of us find the life of Mary and the way the Church has unfolded its meaning intellectually stimulating, it is in church where we learn to act out and enjoy our friendship with the Mother of God. There, with forms provided by the Church, developed and refined over many centuries, we can talk to her and about her out loud, with confidence and with other believers. It must be the feeling a gifted painter experiences when, after study and preparation, he starts painting the portrait of his beloved. The picture makes the knowledge incarnate.

How many holy days does Mary have?

Sixteen in the American calendar. The main ones are the holy days the Church defines as solemnities, meaning holy days of the greatest importance, though not all solemnities are holy days of obligation. (Like Sundays, solemnities always include a second reading, usually from one of the epistles.)

The four solemnities dedicated to Mary are the Solemnity of the Blessed Virgin Mary, celebrating her becoming the Mother of God (January 1); the Annunciation, celebrating Mary's yes to the angel's announcement (March 25, that is, nine months before Christmas); the Assumption, celebrating her entrance, body and soul, into Heaven (August 15); and the Immaculate Conception, celebrating her being conceived without sin (December 8).

Which of these Marian solemnities are holy days of obligation? In the United States, three: the feasts of Mary, Mother of God, the Assumption and the Immaculate Conception. (Holy days of obligation are decided by each country's bishops. The other three days of obligation in the United States are the Ascension, All Saints' Day and Christmas.)

|+| The Blessed Virgin Mary, Mother of God (January 1). Falling on the last day of the Christmas octave, it celebrates her fundamental work as the Mother of God. (An octave is the eight days beginning with a feast day, and a feast on the eighth day is sometimes a way of liturgically "capping off" the feast.) The readings (including the responsorial psalm, which comes after the first reading) are Numbers 6:22–27; Psalm 67:1–5, 7; Galatians 4:4–7; and Luke 2:16–21. An unplanned benefit is that American Catholics begin the secular year dedicating themselves to Mary.

|+| The Assumption (August 15). This feast celebrating the end of Mary's life was started at least in the fifth century and maybe even earlier. It is the oldest Marian feast. Parts of the story traditionally associated with it come from apocryphal books like the fifth-century *Transitus Mariae*. The holy day proclaims the truth that "the Immaculate Mother of God, the ever Virgin

Mary, having completed the course of her earthly life, was assumed body and soul into heavenly glory," as Pope Pius XII defined it in his encyclical *Munificentissimus Deus*, issued in 1950.[1] The readings are 1 Chronicles 15:3–4, 15–16; 16:1–2; Psalm 132:6–7, 9–10, 13–14; 1 Corinthians 15:54b–57; and Luke 11:27–28 for the vigil Mass, and for the Mass during the day Revelation 11:19a; 12:1–6a, 10ab; Psalm 45:10–11, 16; 1 Corinthians 15:20–26; and Luke 1:39–56.

|+|The Immaculate Conception (December 8). A feast celebrating the conception of Mary in the womb of Saint Anne was celebrated in the East as early as the sixth century. Naturally enough, Christians saw Mary's conception as a holy event with meaning for our salvation, even before the doctrine was worked out. Naturally it became the Feast of the Immaculate Conception when that dogma was declared in 1854. The readings are Genesis 3:9–15, 20; Psalm 98:1–4; Ephesians 1:3–6, 11–12; and Luke 1:26–38.

Christmas, or the Nativity of Our Lord, is another holy day of obligation celebrating an event in which Mary is intimately involved, but it is directed to the birth of Christ and so is not included here. The Epiphany, celebrating the wise men's discovery of Jesus, is also not a Marian feast, though Matthew makes a point of saying that the Magi saw the young boy with Mary, His mother (Matthew 2:11).

Besides the three Marian holy days of obligation, what are the other major Marian holy days?

There are thirteen in the calendar for the Catholic Church in the United States. These are the days that either include the Blessed

Virgin Mary in the title or use the Common or Proper for the Blessed Virgin Mary in the lectionary for the Mass. They are classified as solemnities, feasts, memorials and optional memorials, in order of importance.

Five celebrate events in Mary's life, from her birth to her crowning as Queen of Heaven. One celebrates her parents, three a devotion, three one of Mary's later appearances and one the dedication of a church in her honor.

The thirteen are:

|+|Our Lady of Lourdes (February 11, an optional memorial). Mary appeared repeatedly to Saint Bernadette Soubirous in Lourdes, France, in 1858. Mary called herself "the Immaculate Conception," a recently declared dogma of which the uneducated young girl would have been totally unaware. Mary told Bernadette to dig in the mud, and a spring of water began to flow, which continues to be a source of healing for many. The readings for this feast day are Isaiah 66:10–14; Judith 13:18bcde, 19; John 2:1–11.

|+|The Annunciation of the Lord (March 25, a solemnity). Falling, for obvious reasons, nine months before Christmas, the feast celebrates Gabriel's declaration to Mary that she would bear the Savior and her acceptance, as described in Luke's Gospel (1:26–38). The readings are Isaiah 7:10–14; 8:10; Psalm 40:6–10; Hebrews 10:4–10; and Luke 1:26–38.

|+|The Visitation of the Blessed Virgin Mary (May 31, a feast). This feast commemorates Mary's visit with her cousin Elizabeth. Thus its placement in the calendar shortly after the

Annunciation and before the birth of John the Baptist (cele-brated June 24). The readings are Zephaniah 3:14–18a *or* Romans 12:9–16; Isaiah 12:2–3, 4–6 (the psalm response); and Luke 1:39–56.

|+|The Immaculate Heart of the Blessed Virgin Mary (the Saturday following the second Sunday after Pentecost, an optional memorial). In 1942 Pope Pius XIII consecrated the world to the Immaculate Heart of Mary, in response to Our Lady's request of three young children at Fatima, Portugal, in 1917. This devotion focuses on all that Mary's human heart sug-gests: her interior life, her joys and sorrows, her virtues and her love for God and for us. The readings are Isaiah 61:9–11; 1 Samuel 2:1, 4–8 (the psalm response); and Luke 2:41–51.

|+|Our Lady of Mount Carmel (July 16, an optional memorial). In 1251 Our Lady presented a scapular to Saint Simon Stock, general of the Carmelites, and instructed people to wear it and consecrate themselves to her service. The readings are Zechariah 2:14–17; Luke 1:46–55 (the psalm response); and Matthew 12:46–50.

|+|Saints Joachim and Anne (July 26, a memorial). The Church honors the holy parents of the Blessed Virgin Mary, praising them for their child and asking their prayers for our salvation. The readings are Sirach (or Ecclesiasticus) 44:1, 10–15; Psalm 132:11, 13–14, 17–18; and Matthew 13:16–17.

|+|The Dedication of the Basilica of Saint Mary Major (some-times called by its Italian name, *Sancta Maria Maggiore*) in Rome

(August 5, an optional memorial). A thirteenth-century legend, in which snow appeared on this day, popularized this feast under the title "Dedication of the Blessed Virgin Mary of the Snows." The readings are Revelation 21:1–5a; Judith 13:18–19 (the responsorial psalm); and Luke 11:27–28.

|+|The Queenship of the Blessed Virgin Mary (August 22, a memorial). This feast comes eight days after the Feast of the Assumption and emphasizes the place in Heaven God has given Mary. The readings are Isaiah 9:1–6; Psalm 113:1–8; and Luke 1:26–38.

|+|The Nativity (or birth) of the Blessed Virgin Mary (September 8, a feast). Nine months after the Feast of the Immaculate Conception, the Church celebrates Mary's birth to Joachim and Anna. The celebration began in the East in the fourth century and grew in observance and popularity. Although we have no certain information about Mary's birth, the Church is sure, and celebrates on this day, that God had specially prepared her to be the Mother of the Savior. The readings are Micah 5:1–4a or Romans 8:28–30; Psalm 13:5–66; and Matthew 1:1–16, 18–23 or 1:18–23.

|+|Our Lady of Sorrows (September 15, a memorial). This feast immediately follows that of the Exaltation of the Holy Cross. Mary's seven sorrows include the words of Simeon at the presentation of Jesus in the temple, the flight into Egypt, the loss of the twelve-year-old Jesus in Jerusalem, meeting Jesus on his way to Calvary, standing at the foot of the cross watching Him

die, His being taken from the cross and His burial. The readings for this feast are Hebrews 5:7–9; Psalm 31:2–6, 15–16, 20; and John 19:25–27 *or* Luke 2:33–35.

|+|Our Lady of the Rosary (October 7, a memorial). This feast commemorates the victory over Muslim invaders at the Gulf of Lepanto in 1571, which may have saved Europe from being conquered and subjugated. Pope Pius V had prescribed public prayer for deliverance, and a rosary procession at a church in Rome was pleading for divine help during the very hour of the battle. The readings are Acts 1:12–14; Luke 1:46–55 (the responsorial psalm); and Luke 1:26–38.

|+|The Presentation of the Blessed Virgin Mary (November 21, a memorial). This feast marks Mary's dedication in the temple by her parents Saints Joachim and Anna. This is another feast for which we have no certain information, although with Mary's relative Elizabeth being a descendent of the high priest Aaron and Mary's Jewish piety implying pious parents, that she would be specially dedicated to God makes sense. The readings are Zechariah 2:14–17; Luke 1:46–55 (the responsorial psalm); and Matthew 12:46–50.

|+|Our Lady of Guadalupe (December 12, a feast). This is a feast celebrated in the United States but not in the universal Roman calendar, for Mary is the patron saint of the Americas. The readings are Zechariah 2:14–17 or Revelation 11:19a; 12:1–6a, 10ab; Judith 13:18bcde, 19 (the responsorial psalm); and Luke 1:26–38 *or* 1:39–47.

In addition to these thirteen holy days, the Presentation of Our Lord in the Temple (February 2, a feast) might be included because it has also been known as the Purification of Mary. Jewish mothers were expected to undergo a ritual bath, or *mikvah*, for purification forty days after bearing a child, and the feast comes forty days after Christmas. The readings are Malachi 3:1–4; Psalm 24:7–10; Hebrews 2:14–18; and Luke 2:22–32 or 22–40.

Mass on Saturday is also often celebrated in Mary's honor.

Are there any more holy days for Mary?

Many. They don't have the official status of those listed in the Church's calendar but are observed by many devout Catholics. Parishes with many members of Irish descent might celebrate the Feast of Our Lady of Knock on August 21, for example, the title referring to Mary's appearance in the town of Knock in 1879. Mary is the patron saint of Ireland.

Among the other feasts—this is a representative but not comprehensive list—are the Espousal of the Virgin Mary (January 23), Our Lady of Good Counsel (April 26), Mary, Help of Christians (May 24), Our Lady, Queen of the Apostles (the Saturday after the Ascension), Our Lady of Perpetual Help (June 27), Our Lady of the Angels (August 2), the Most Holy Name of Mary (September 12) and the Patronage of Our Lady (November 11).

How is Mary mentioned in the liturgy for the Mass on Marian feast days?

In these liturgies Mary always is invoked or proclaimed in relation to the work of her son. The set parts given in the Common for the feasts ("Common" meaning the special prayers and readings for that kind of day) are not as exuberantly Marian as one might expect, though of course the hymns, prayers and homily may be.

For example, in the Common of the Blessed Virgin Mary for Advent, the Opening Prayer begins, "Father, in your plan for our salvation your Word became man, announced by an angel and born of the Virgin Mary. May we who believe that she is the Mother of God receive the help of her prayers. We ask this through our Lord Jesus Christ, your Son." The Prayer After Communion reads, "Lord our God, / may the sacraments we receive / show us your forgiveness and love. / May we who honor the mother of your Son / be saved by his coming among us as man, / for he is Lord for ever and ever."[2]

One of the Commons for Masses in Ordinary Time begins, "Lord, / take away the sins of your people. / May the prayers of Mary the mother of your Son help us, / for alone and unaided we cannot hope to please you." The Prayer Over the Gifts includes the lines "Father, / the birth of Christ your Son / deepened the virgin mother's love for you, / and increased her holiness. / May the humanity of Christ / give us courage in our weakness; / may it free us from our sins."[3]

Other services can be more overtly Marian. In Morning Prayer of the Common for the Blessed Virgin Mary, for example, the first antiphon says, "Blessed are you, O Mary, for the world's salvation came forth from you; now in glory, you rejoice for ever with the Lord. Intercede for us with your Son." The second one says, "You are the glory of Jerusalem, the joy of Israel; you are the fairest honor of our race," and the third, "O Virgin Mary, how great your cause for joy; God found you worthy to bear Christ our Savior."[4]

Each Marian feast has antiphons fitting the reason for the feast. The first antiphon for the Immaculate Conception, for example, reads, "O Mother, how pure you are, you are untouched by sin; yours was the privilege to carry God within you."[5]

Does Saint Joseph have a holy day?

Yes, two. The first, the Feast of Saint Joseph, Husband of the Blessed Virgin Mary, is observed on March 19, and it is a solemnity—not surprisingly, since Joseph is patron of the universal Church. The readings are 2 Samuel 7:4–5a, 12–14a, 16; Psalm 89:1–4, 26, 28; Romans 4:13, 16–18, 22; and Matthew 1:16, 18–21, 24a or Luke 2:41–51a.

The second, the Feast of Saint Joseph the Worker, is observed on May 1, and it is an optional memorial. The readings are Genesis 1:26–2:3 *or* Colossians 3:14–15, 17, 23–24; Psalm 90:2–4, 12–14, 16; and Matthew 13:54–58.

What is happening in the liturgy on the Marian feast days?

In *Behold Your Mother*, the American bishops put it this way:

> When we celebrate the memory of Mary in the liturgy, we join together in a present liturgical "moment" the past and the future—what Mary once was on earth, as the Gospels show her, and the future, our reunion with Mary and the saints, including the uncanonized saints of our own families, reunited in the risen Lord.[6]

In the liturgy, whether at Mass or another service, we look with gratitude at what God has done in Mary, and done in Mary for us, and praise Him for it. And we look with hope and gratitude to what He will do for us and praise Him for it. When we praise Mary—when we say, for example, "You are the glory of Jerusalem, the joy of Israel"—we are also praising God, who made Mary who and what she is.

CHAPTER FIVE

MARY'S TITLES

In an old movie called *Moscow on the Hudson*, a Soviet musician defects in New York City. His host takes him to an American grocery store, where he, accustomed to empty Soviet stores and overwhelmed with all the choices he can make, shakes wildly for a few seconds and then passes out.

Those new to the Church may feel similarly overwhelmed by the great number and diversity of Mary's titles. They have known her only as "Mary," or in more formal traditions as "the Blessed Virgin Mary" or maybe as "Our Lady," but that is about it. The exuberance and apparent chaos of Catholic speech disconcerts them or even repels them, as if someone who loved classic smooth lawns with well-trimmed shrubs and carefully arranged flower beds was suddenly thrown into the Amazon jungle. It's all too much.

But it isn't really. The multiplication of titles follows from the Catholic knowledge of who Mary is and what God has done and is doing in and through her. For example, Catholics everywhere feel that they know her, that through their brother Jesus she's their mother, and they honor her with a child's natural devotion. She becomes local, a mother of particular people and a woman of particular places, while remaining universal. And so all over the world we find churches and shrines called "Our Lady of This" and "Our Lady of That," but the Lady each claims is the same Lady.

How you respond to this depends on how you think about it. You could see it as all chaos and confusion, but you could also see it as a great sign of God's love for all mankind and the reconciliation of peoples in which they remain themselves. It's not like a crowded street, with everyone going his own way, but like a block party in a multiethnic neighborhood, with everyone sharing from his own tradition and everyone enjoying the differences.

The great number and diversity of Marian titles is, in other words, a very Catholic thing, an expression of many of the good things God gives us through the Church and through Our Lady.

How many titles does Mary have?
More than we can count, since Christian imagination and devotion have found myriad ways to describe Mary and her work. The prayer the Litany of Loreto, for example, includes fifty-one.

Of titles that might be called official—that is, titles used in magisterial documents—sixteen are listed in the index to the *Catechism of the Catholic Church* under the heading "titles of Mary." They are Advocate, Help, Benefactress, Mediatrix, Ever Virgin, Full of Grace, Handmaid of the Lord, *Hodigitria* (a Greek word meaning "She shows the way"), Immaculate, Mother of

Christ, Mother of the Church, Mother of God, Mother of the Living, the New Eve, *Panagia* (another Greek word, meaning "All Holy") and Seat of Wisdom.[1]

The popes have used many others. In his encyclicals Pope John Paul II uses the titles Daughter of Sion, Daughter of Your Son, Morning Star, Mother of the Church, Mother of God, Mother of the Living, Mother of Mercy, New Eve, Queen of the Universe, Seat of Wisdom, Spouse of the Holy Spirit, Star of the Sea and others.[2] In just one section of his encyclical *Redemptoris Mater*, speaking of Russian icons (a section I chose at random to illustrate the range of images upon which the Catholic can call), he calls Mary the image of divine beauty, the abode of eternal wisdom, the figure of one who prays, the prototype of contemplation and the image of glory.[3]

To give another example, in just the first ten sections of his *Cultus Marialis*, Pope Paul VI calls Mary not only by her name but also the Mother of God, the Mother of Christ, the Mother of the Church, the Virgin Mother, the Mother of the Lord, the True Seat of Wisdom, the True Mother of the King, the Holy Mother, the Queen of Peace, the True Mother of the Living, the True Ark of the Covenant and True Temple of God, Queen, Our Lady, the Ever-Virgin Mother of Jesus Christ and the Blessed of the Most High (this last a reference to Luke 1:28). And this list doesn't include the titles he mentions when discussing feasts celebrating her appearances and devotions, like Our Lady of Lourdes, Our Lady of Mount Carmel and Our Lady of the Rosary.[4]

Then there are the titles presented to define or declare Mary's role in particular circumstances. In *Ineffabilis Deus*, the apostolic constitution that declares the doctrine of the Immaculate

Conception, for example, Pius IX refers to Mary as the "Reparatrix of the first parents."5

Why so many titles?

For two reasons, I think.

First, Mary has been given so many titles in Christian devotion because people naturally think up new names for someone they love, to try to express her excellence and virtue. Love is expansive and exuberant. Love makes up names.

Second, the proliferation of titles suggests the depths and the complexity of Mary's place in God's economy of salvation. She has many titles because God has used her in many ways.

Four titles from the Litany of Loreto illustrate both reasons. "Ark of the Covenant" compares Mary to the ark, which was for the Jews of the Old Testament, especially those wandering in the wilderness on the way to the Promised Land, God's special dwelling place. (We looked at this title at more length in the questions in chapter two on the New Testament's use of the Old Testament.) "Tower of Ivory" presents her as both strong and pure and beautiful. To call Mary "Gate of Heaven" emphasizes that through her came the Savior, who brings us to Heaven, and reminds us of her continuing place in our salvation by bringing us to her son. Referring to the star that shines brightly before the sun rises, the title "Morning Star" reminds us that Mary shone as a herald of the Light of the World she would soon bear— and that she shines still.

What titles do Church documents use?

Primarily "the Blessed Virgin Mary" but also "the Blessed Virgin." In the documents of the Second Vatican Council, she seems to be called "the Blessed Virgin" more than she is called by name.

What kinds of titles does Mary have?

Broadly speaking, two: what might be called her "name titles" and her "function titles." The first name her, the second proclaim something she is or does. Some are the products of Christian reflection and devotion, others are official titles given by the magisterium, though the magisterium often ratified titles that the spiritual instincts of the people had created.

The "name titles" always refer to Mary in relation to her son. They include titles like "Mother of God," "the Blessed Mother," "the Virgin Mother" and even "Our Lady," which refers indirectly to her son because she is only Our Lady (as in "the lady of the manor") because she is the Mother of our Lord.

The "function titles" also refer to Mary in relation to her son but by what she is or does because she is the Mother of her son. They include titles like "Help of Christians," "Mediatrix," "Immaculate Conception" and "Seat of Wisdom."

What are the titles beginning "Mother of"?

Besides the obvious ones, like "Mother of God" and others declaring her relation to her son, here are a few: Mother of Christians, Mother of Divine Grace, Mother of Good Counsel, Mother of Men, Mother of the Church, Mother of the Mystical Body and Mother of Wisdom.

What are the titles beginning "Our Lady of"?

Too many to list. Here is a representative selection: Our Lady of Charity; Our Lady of Consolation; Our Lady of Good Counsel; Our Lady of Good Help; Our Lady of Good Remedy; Our Lady of Grace; Our Lady of High Grace; Our Lady of Mercy; Our Lady of

Peace; Our Lady of Perpetual Help; Our Lady of Prompt Succor; Our Lady of Providence; Our Lady of Ransom; Our Lady of Safe Travel; Our Lady of Sorrows; Our Lady of Tears; Our Lady of Victory; Our Lady of the Assumption; Our Lady of the Cape; Our Lady of the Hermits; Our Lady of the Highways; Our Lady of the Holy Souls; Our Lady of the Immaculate Conception; Our Lady of the Incarnation; Our Lady of the Milk and Happy Delivery; Our Lady of the Presentation; Our Lady of the Rosary; Our Lady of the Scapular; Our Lady of the Snows; Our Lady of the Valley; Our Lady of the Wayside; Our Lady Who Appeared.

And then there are all the titles that relate Mary to a particular place at which she appeared (of which there are many), like Our Lady of Guadalupe and Our Lady of Lourdes. Others relate to a devotion, like Our Lady of the Holy Rosary and Our Lady of the Miraculous Medal.

And then there are other "of" titles, like Our Lady, Gate of Heaven; Our Lady, Help of Christians; Our Lady, Mother of the Church; Our Lady, Queen of All Saints; Our Lady, Queen of the Apostles; and Our Lady, Mediatrix of All Grace.

What does "Mediatrix" mean, and how does it relate to Christ's being our mediator with the Father?

This title particularly upsets some people. Mary is a mediator between God and man, though not in a way that denies the mediation of Christ. She mediates only because Jesus is *the* mediator and has given her a role in His mediation.

Indeed every Christian has a share in Christ's mediation, in the same way that priests share in Jesus' unique priesthood. Why else would we pray the intercessions at Mass, but that God wants us to have a role in His governance of the world? Why else would Saint Paul tell Saint Timothy that everyone should intercede for others, just before declaring that Jesus is the one mediator between God and men (see 1 Timothy 2:1–6)?

As the Mother of God, immaculately conceived and assumed into Heaven, Mary has a unique mediating role, the same in kind as that given to the rest of us but perfect in degree and execution. As the Fathers of the Second Vatican Council explained in *Lumen Gentium*, "By her maternal charity, she cares for the brethren of her Son, who still journey on earth surrounded by dangers and difficulties, until they are led into their blessed home."[6] This is why she is called "Mediatrix," as well as names like "Advocate."

Why do some writers, including some saints, call Mary divine?

The exuberant language about Mary that some writers have used can alarm more sedate moderns and offend Protestant Christians, who on hearing it accuse Catholics of "Mariolatry." Saint Louis de Montfort, for example, wrote that "it would even be easier to separate all the angels and saints from you [Jesus] than Mary; for she loves you ardently, and glorifies you more perfectly than all your other creatures put together."[7]

The saints who used this kind of language wrote with depths and subtleties that can't be expounded here (if at all, by anyone else), but a simple answer to this question is that anything they say of Mary is true only because of what Christ did for her and in no sense erases the distinction between God and creature. They were writing for people who understood that. The firmer a knowledge you have of who Mary is, the more exuberant and expressive can be your language, precisely because you know where the lines are.

In using the word *divine*, for example, Saint Louis and others are exploring what Mary's unique intimacy with her son meant. And they are not using language previously unknown. In fact they are using biblical language. The psalmist describes God as saying to His people, "You are gods" (Psalm 82:6), a phrase Jesus quotes (see John 10:34–36). Saint Peter wrote that through Christ we all can become "partakers of the divine nature" (2 Peter 1:4).

Developing this point, the fourth-century Father Saint Athanasius famously declared in his *On the Incarnation* that God became man so that man might become God.[8] Saint Louis's language is not heretical or even imprecise, or even new.

To speak personally for a moment, I have always found that language that disturbed me when I first heard it eventually made sense as I grew in my faith and tried docilely to understand what the saints were telling me, even though they used language very, very far from the language I knew when I came to the Church. Often I saw that the language was the best or even only way of saying something that could not be said otherwise, and that it proclaimed some new (new to me, that is) aspect of the gospel. In this case, I would be more comfortable with the simple term *godly*, which is almost a synonym but does not point me to something that *divine* conveys.

Why would we call Mary Our Blessed Mother when she was Jesus' mother?

We know Mary is "blessed" because the angel Gabriel said so, as did Mary's cousin Elizabeth. But the reason is not just the obvious one of her unique relation to the Son of God. Long ago Saint Augustine noted that "men are not blessed for this reason, that they are united by nearness of flesh unto just and holy men, but that, by obeying and following, they cleave unto their doctrine and conduct. Therefore Mary is more blessed in receiving the faith of Christ, than in conceiving the flesh of Christ."[9]

We can call Mary our mother first because she is Jesus' mother, and as the mother of Christ she is by extension the mother of the members of the Body of Christ. As *Lumen Gentium* explains it, quoting Saint Augustine, she is the mother of Christians because "she has by her charity joined in bringing about the birth of believers in the Church, who are members of its head."[10]

But as the American bishops noted in *Behold Your Mother*, there is more to Mary's motherhood than bearing Christ (see Ephesians 1:22–23). Because she had such perfect faith in God, "she became the perfect example of what the Gospels mean by 'spiritual motherhood.'"

Why was Mary called the Mother of God?

Christians started using the title very early in the Church's life, but it was not made official until the Council of Ephesus in AD 431, first in the form of *Theotokos*, meaning "the one who gave birth to God." As described in the chapter on doctrine, the bishops gathered there declared the *Theotokos* because a leading bishop and theologian named Nestorius denied that Jesus was a single person, God and man both, and expressed this by pointedly calling Mary simply the "Christ-bearer."

So the perhaps startling title the council gave Mary was in fact a statement about her son, the Fathers of the council arguing that if Jesus is who He is, then this is who Mary is. If the human being Mary is the Mother of God, Jesus is indivisibly man and God. Because people kept trying to diminish either Jesus' humanity or his divinity, orthodox Christians soon started speaking of Mary even more boldly as the "Mother of God," a title affirmed by the fifth General Council, held in Chalcedon in 451.

Why is Mary called our "Advocate"?

It is an ancient title, because Christians very early saw that someone that God so exalted would be in a unique position to intercede with her son and the Father. It was especially popular in the Middle Ages, appearing often in the writings of Saint Bernard of Clairvaux (now a doctor of the Church) in the early twelfth century. We use it today in the prayer and hymn *Salve Regina* ("Hail, Holy Queen").

The Church has been careful to distinguish Mary's advocacy from the mediation of her son, whom Saint Paul describes as "the one mediator between God and men" (1 Timothy 2:5). A reader of all the magisterial documents on Mary would be struck, I think, by how often and how carefully the authors make sure that the reader knows that everything we know about Mary (and the saints) points to Christ.

In the chapter on Mary in *Lumen Gentium*, the fathers of the Second Vatican Council insist several times, almost monotonously, that she is who she is, and is not God. In describing her motherly "duty" to men, they say it "in no way obscures or diminishes this unique mediation of Christ, but rather shows His power. For all the salvific influences of the Blessed Virgin on men originates, not from some inner necessity, but from the divine pleasure."[12]

Put a little differently, she is who she is and does what she does because God loved her and loved us. She is our advocate because God gave her the position.

What is meant by calling Mary the "Queen of Heaven"?

Pope Pius XII explained this when he established the Feast of the Blessed Virgin Mary, Queen, in his Encyclical *Ad Caeli Reginam*, issued in 1954. Noting that Scripture speaks of Jesus as the eternal ruler, a prince and the King of Kings, he writes that "when Christians reflected upon the intimate connection that obtains between a mother and a son, they readily acknowledged the supreme royal dignity of the Mother of God."

Mary, he continues,

> is a Queen, since she bore a son who, at the very moment of His conception, because of the hypostatic union of the human nature with the Word, was also as man King and Lord of all things. So with complete justice Saint John Damascene could write: "When she became Mother of the Creator, she truly became Queen of every creature."[13]

But she is not Queen in herself and for herself. At her assumption the Lord exalted her as "Queen of the universe," *Lumen*

Gentium tells us, "that she might be the more thoroughly con-formed to her Son, the Lord of lords."[14]

Don't titles like "Advocate" and "Mediatrix" confuse Mary's place with her son's?

Some non-Catholics have charged that the Catholic treatment of Mary, and particularly the use of titles like "Advocate" and "Mediatrix," denies the plain teaching of Scripture about Jesus, like the statement of Saint Paul just quoted. But they badly mis-understand what the Church means.

Mary does what any of us might do for another, but she does so from a position no one else has. She speaks for us as a crea-ture, but a creature who has been given unique privileges. Mary's work of advocacy and mediation is somewhat like that of a queen who speaks to the king for a commoner, who could and has made his own petitions to the king. She is not claiming to be the king, and she is not doing anything another of the king's subjects could not do, but because the king has made her queen, she appeals to the king with a unique authority and effect. The commoner will appeal to the king, but he will naturally also appeal to the queen to speak to the king on his behalf.

It is possible to think of an arrangement in which everyone speaks to God without mediation of any sort, but this is not the arrangement He has given us. He chose to bring His Son into the world through a human mother. He chose that His Son would establish a Church through which the men His Son redeemed would participate in the work of redemption. He chose to give us our sacred writings through human writers and to communicate his truths through a magisterium, and to listen to our prayers for each other. He chose to assume Mary into Heaven and to give us a way to speak to her.

As the bishops said in *Lumen Gentium*, "The unique mediation of the Redeemer does not exclude but rather gives rise to a manifold cooperation which is but a sharing in this one source."[15] That is the interdependent life of the family, in which everyone advocates and mediates for everyone else, and Mary, fittingly, does so perfectly and universally.

CHAPTER SIX

MARIAN DEVOTIONS, PRAYERS AND APPARITIONS

When well more than a billion people in hundreds of cultures over two thousand years all turn to the same mother as their own, they will develop a startling variety of devotions. These will be revised and refined over the years, as people use them and they spread to other cultures, and the Church's theologians and bishops evaluate them. Some will die out, some will be condemned, and some will be naturally selected because they are especially profound or useful or because they appeal to most Catholics across cultures.

Catholic devotion to Mary is exuberant and inventive for the reason I gave at the beginning of the last chapter: It develops from an ever deepening knowledge of who she is and what God is doing in and through her, and from the belief that Mary belongs to every Catholic, because her son became incarnate for everyone. She has lots and lots of devoted children trying to express their love for her, many of them clever and creative.

Here I can only list the very most important prayers and devotions. The Church offers many more. A priest told me about one particularly beautiful and meaningful devotion, of which I'd never heard, just as I was finishing this book, for example. A newlywed virgin presents white flowers to Mary at a shrine, symbolically exchanging virginity for motherhood as she asks the intercession of she who was both Virgin and Mother.

What is the point of Marian devotion?

To know the Savior better and to be more like Him. The classic way of putting it is that greater love and knowledge of Mary leads to greater love and knowledge of her son, and vice versa.

Marian devotion works out this way, I think, for the same reason Marian understanding developed in the early Church. The Christian meets Jesus and gets to know Him better, and as he does begins to wonder about those around Jesus, and most of all about His mother. As he gets to know her better, he finds that everything he learns about her points him back to her son.

He learns that she was conceived without the stain of original sin and is thus perfectly lovely and lovable, but only because the Father prepared her in this way to be the mother of His Son. And so the Christian turns back to the Son, loving our Lord all the more for what He did for His mother. His love for Jesus increased, his love for Mary increases also, and he looks at her yet more closely. And so on, in a circle that as it turns pulls him ever further into the love of God.

This is why Pope Paul VI said that such devotion "has to be regarded as a help which of its very nature leads men to Christ."[1]

You can't love Mary only for herself. That makes no sense.

The Hail Mary gives an example of this dynamic, this back and forth between praise for the Mother and praise for the Son. The first half begins, "Hail Mary, full of grace, the Lord is with thee," declaring that Mary is full of grace because she is filled with the Lord, and continues, "Blessed art thou among women," blessed because she was given the privilege of bearing the Lord. It finishes with "And blessed is the fruit of your womb, Jesus," capping off the prayer by pointing directly to the Lord.

The second half begins, "Holy Mary, Mother of God," establishing her status in relation to the Lord, and finishes, "Pray for us sinners now and at the hour of our death," a plea we can make in confidence because she is everything the prayer has just declared her to be.

The Hail Mary is a Marian devotion but also a declaration of praise to the Lord. Like every true Marian devotion, it includes as a kind of footnote to every phrase "because of Jesus."

Can one be a faithful Catholic without Marian devotion?

No. For three reasons.

First, devotion to Mary is part of the practice of the Church. It is what the faithful Christian does. In *Behold Your Mother* the bishops call it "the joyful duty of all of us."[2]

In the United States the feasts of Mary the Mother of God, the Assumption, and the Immaculate Conception are all holy days of obligation, days whose observance is so important that you must disrupt your schedule and get to Mass. Popes have regularly encouraged the saying of the rosary and indeed spoken of it as a normal and expected part of the Christian life.

Second, devotion to Mary grows naturally, and should grow inevitably, from a love of Jesus and the desire to live the life He wants. It grows not simply from the normal human instinct to love those who are loved by someone we love, especially their parents, though that should not be denigrated. It grows also from our deepening knowledge of what God has done in Mary.

Third, devotion to Mary expresses, indeed makes practical for us, our belief in the communion of saints. They are available to us, wanting for us the joy they have in Heaven and praying to God for our needs. Naturally enough, we look to the first among the saints for her help.

The point of Marian devotion, in other words, is to live the Catholic life as well as we can. This means going ever more deeply into the mystery of Christ, to become saintlier, more conformed to His image, by following Mary's example and by turning to her for help and comfort.

There is a danger, which should be mentioned in passing, of reducing the Christian life to a set of rules to follow and reducing Mary to a good example or model of someone who obeyed those rules. A personal devotion, a love for the person of Mary, helps guard against this deadening idea of the spiritual life. Most of us will find pleasing Mary our mother by following her son easier and richer than trying to satisfy a list of rules.

Does devotion to Mary detract from our devotion to Christ?

No, for the reason given in the first question of this chapter. There is the danger that someone might love the mother more than the Son, but the danger is not as great as the critics of

Marian devotion assert. They need to understand the way Marian devotion actually works.

Think of meeting the parents of a war hero, especially one who gave his life to save others. You might praise them for raising such a son, but they will turn the praise to him, telling you about his virtues, his kindness and courage as a child, the sacrifices he made for others even then, hoping to help you love him more. And you will begin to love him more because those who knew him so well encouraged you to, but you will also love *them* more because they praise their son. An outsider—an old friend of the war hero, say—hearing only your praise for the parents, might think you'd missed the point and were praising the wrong person, not realizing that your praise for them reflected a greater and deeper praise for the hero.

Christians since the beginning of serious Marian devotion have been careful to emphasize Mary's subordination to her son. In fact, they have said it so often that the reader begins to expect it. In the fifth century Saint Ambrose put it nicely: "Mary was the temple of God, not the god of the temple."[3]

Of course there will be abuses and misunderstandings, because we are sinners. But Marian devotion is self-correcting. At some point you will realize that the excessive adoration makes no sense and dishonors the one you intend to honor. And if you don't, the mainstream of the Church and her magisterium will correct you.

How is Mary spoken of in Christian devotion?
In as many ways as human creativity and insight can find. Let me give one example from Saint Peter Damian's sermon on the Feast of the Epiphany.

Men were living in the darkness of sin, the saint explained, when the star over Bethlehem declared "the Light." He continued: "There was a star in the sky, a star on earth and the Sun in the manger. The star in the sky was that bright heavenly body; the star on earth, the Virgin Mary; the Sun in the manger, Christ our Lord." Mary is like a star because

> A star...has four main characteristics: it has the nature of fire, it is bright and clear, it sends forth a ray and it shines in the night. ...And she has sent forth from herself a ray which pierces to the secret places of the heart and searches the heart and the reins; this is the living Word of God, quick and powerful, and sharper than any two-edged sword.... [S]he has sent forth from herself that ray "which lighteth every man that cometh into the world." And just as the ray issues from the star without destroying the star's integrity, so the Son came forth from the Virgin while her virginity remained inviolate.[4]

One difference a reader might notice is that modern Marian devotion may be more overtly biblical than that of the past (not necessarily more biblical, mind you, but more overtly so). Pope Paul VI noted that the "texts of prayers and chants should draw their inspiration and their wording from the Bible, and above all...devotion to the Virgin should be imbued with the great themes of the Christian message."[5]

How is devotion to Mary (and the other saints) different from devotion to God?

The Church distinguishes worship or adoration (*latria* in Greek) from veneration (*dulia*). Only God can be worshipped and adored, but Mary and the other saints can and indeed ought to be venerated. We honor and respect those greater than we, but in doing so we honor the God who made them what they are, as explained already.

As the bishops at the Council of Trent (session 25) put it, churches should have images of Mary and the other saints, and "due honor and veneration are to be given them...because the honor which is shown them is referred to the prototypes which those images represent; [so] that by the images...we kiss, and before which we uncover the head, and prostrate ourselves, we adore Christ; and we venerate the saints, whose similitude they bear." The bishops noted that doing so did not mean that "any divinity, or virtue, is believed to be in [these images], on account of which they are to be worshipped."[6]

Veneration is not just high respect and admiration, such as we might have for any hero or great man, but a kind of submission as well. We see the saints as those in whom our Lord speaks and whose lives reveal to us something about Him. They are people we should follow, but we follow them and venerate them because they are so like Christ. They are our better brothers and sisters, to whom we naturally talk and whom we naturally praise, but whose heroism leads us to think of our Father, who made them heroes.

Our love for the saints in Heaven, *Lumen Gentium* says, "by its very nature tends toward and terminates in Christ who is the 'crown of all saints,' and through Him, in God Who is wonderful in His saints and magnified in them."[7]

Mary has one distinction here: alone among the saints she is due *hyperdulia*, or very great veneration, because of her place in the economy of salvation and her intimacy with the Lord. This is still not worship but a recognition that she is, through the work of Christ Himself, of all mankind most like Christ.

What role do Marian devotions have in our relations with other Christians?

A difficult one, particularly with our Protestant friends who, as we discussed in chapter three, reject most Marian doctrine and therefore almost every Marian devotion.

Lumen Gentium tells theologians and preachers—and the rest of us as well, presumably—to "carefully refrain from whatever might by word or deed lead the separated brethren or any others whatsoever into error about the true doctrine of the Church."[8] This warning seems to work in two directions: on the one hand, we should not exaggerate our devotion so that Protestant and Orthodox Christians think we believe something other than we do, but on the other hand, we should not diminish our devotion so they think we believe less than we do.

Mary is not to be used as a weapon, but neither is she to be set aside out of deference to the feelings of others. And practically speaking, the fellowship we would gain with the Protestants by reducing our devotion to Mary we would lose with the Orthodox.

For what sorts of things can we ask Mary?

Any need or godly desire.

But some needs are particularly appropriate for her: purity, for example, and the courage and will to do what God asks of us.

For help in raising children or help in facing the death of a child. In these cases and many others, Mary has been there, so to speak.

Is there a standard Marian devotion?

Not really, though the Church encourages everyone to say the rosary and the Angelus daily. Different people will find different devotions natural to them, and some more helpful than others. The Church has approved many forms, notes *Lumen Gentium*, which vary "according to the conditions of time and place, and the nature and ingenuity of the faithful."[9] As with most things, there are "cooler" and "hotter" versions, but they all express a believer's love of the Mother of God.

What is devotion to the Immaculate Heart of Mary?

It is a devotion to Mary's heart—her physical heart—taken as a symbol of her sinlessness and her love for the Lord and for us. A common prayer in this devotion is a prayer to the Virgin of Fatima, who is described as "Mother of mercy, Queen of heaven and earth, refuge of sinners."

The devotion begins with consecration to the Immaculate Heart, a renewal of one's baptismal and confirmation promises and the promise to "live as good Christians—faithful to God, the Church and the Holy Father." In particular the one making the devotion promises to pray the rosary, partake of the Mass, "work for the conversion of sinners" and spread devotion to Mary, all in order to hasten the coming of the kingdom.[10]

What is the rosary?

The word *rosary* refers both to the string of beads used in saying the prayers and to the prayer itself.

The typical set of rosary beads has five sets of ten beads together and one by itself (called a "decade"), set in a circle and bound by a clasp, which often has a picture of Mary on it, with a string with five beads ending in a crucifix hanging down from it. The beads both help you keep track of where you are in the prayer and (at least for those among us with ADHD) help you concentrate by giving your hands and body something to do.

You begin praying the rosary by holding the crucifix and reciting the Apostles' Creed. On the five beads next to the crucifix, you say an Our Father, three Hail Marys (usually for growth in faith, hope and charity) and then a Glory Be ("Glory be to the Father and to the Son and to the Holy Spirit. As it was in the beginning, is now and ever shall be, world without end, amen"). For each decade you say one Our Father and ten Hail Marys, one on each of the ten beads, finishing with a Glory Be. Usually you just go around the rosary once and finish with a variety of prayers, including the Fatima Prayer and the *Salve Regina* ("Hail, Holy Queen") (both described in the answer to the next question).

While praying each decade you meditate on a "mystery," one mystery for each decade. There are four sets of mysteries: the joyful, the luminous, the sorrowful and the glorious. Pope John Paul II added the luminous mysteries in 2002, in his Apostolic Letter on the Rosary, *Rosarium Virginis Mariae*.[11]

The joyful mysteries reflect on Jesus' conception, birth and childhood, while the luminous mysteries reflect on five events in Jesus' life: His baptism, the miracle at the wedding in Cana, His proclaiming of the kingdom of God, the Transfiguration and His institution of the Eucharist. The sorrowful mysteries reflect on His passion and death, beginning with his suffering in the garden and ending with the crucifixion. The glorious mysteries begin with His Resurrection and Ascension and move to the descent of the Holy Spirit at Pentecost and Mary's assumption and crowning as Queen of Heaven.

What are the major Marian prayers?
Though in Marian devotion one man's "major" can be another man's "minor," several prayers are said widely and often. There are many, many prayers, but here are the prayers with which the Catholic should be most familiar.

|+| The *Sub Tuum Praesidium* (second or third century). A simple prayer, but one that shows how early Christians turned to Mary. It goes:

> We fly to your patronage, O holy Mother of God.
> Despise not our petitions in our necessities,
> but deliver us always from all dangers, O glorious and blessed Virgin. [12]

|+| *Ave Maris Stella* (ninth or tenth century). This is a hymn sung at Evening Prayer on Marian feasts.

> Hail, O star of the ocean,
> God's own Mother blest,

ever sinless Virgin,
gate of heavenly rest.

Taking that sweet Ave,
which from Gabriel came,
please confirm within us,
changing Eve's name.

Break the sinners' fetters,
make our blindness day,
chase all evils from us,
for all blessings pray.

Show thyself a Mother;
may the Word divine,
born for us thine Infant,
hear our prayers through thine.

Virgin all excelling,
mildest of the mild,
freed from guilt preserve us
meek and undefiled.

Keep our lives all spotless,
make our way secure,
till we find in Jesus,
joy forevermore.

Praise to God the Father,
honor to the Son,
in the Holy Spirit,
be the glory one. Amen.[13]

|+|*Regina Caeli* (tenth to twelfth century). It replaces the Angelus (given below) during Easter season.

Queen of Heaven, rejoice, alleluia:
For He Whom you merited to bear, alleluia,
Has risen as He said, alleluia.
Pray for us to God, alleluia.

V: Rejoice and be glad, O Virgin Mary, alleluia.
R: Because the Lord is truly risen, alleluia.

Let us pray. O God, Who by the resurrection of your Son, our Lord Jesus Christ, granted joy to the whole world: grant, we beseech Thee, that through the intercession of the Virgin Mary, His mother, we may lay hold of the joys of eternal life. Through the same Jesus Christ our Lord. Amen.

|+|*Alma Redemptoris Mater* (eleventh century):

Mother benign of our redeeming Lord,
Star of the sea and portal of the skies,
Unto thy fallen people help afford—
Fallen but striving still anew to rise.

You who did once, while wondering worlds adored,
Bear your Creator, Virgin then as now,
O by your holy joy at Gabriel's word,
Pity the sinners who before you bow.[14]

|+|*Salve Regina* (eleventh century):

Hail, holy Queen, Mother of Mercy;

hail, our life, our sweetness, and our hope.

To you do we cry, poor banished children of Eve.

To you do we send up our sighs, mourning and weeping in
this valley of tears.

Turn then, most gracious advocate, your eyes of mercy
toward us.

And after this our exile, show unto us the blessed fruit of
your womb, Jesus.

O clement, O loving, O sweet Virgin Mary.

V: Pray for us, O holy Mother of God.

R: That we may be made worthy of the promises of Christ.

|+|*Ave Regina Caelorum* (twelfth century).

Hail, O Queen of Heaven enthroned! Hail, by angels
mistress owned!

Root of Jesse, Gate of Morn, when the world's true Light
was born:

Glorious Virgin, joy to you, loveliest whom in Heaven they
view,

fairest where all are fair, plead with Christ our sins to
spare.[15]

|+| *Stabat Mater* (fourteenth century). This hymn describes Mary's faithfulness at the foot of the cross. It is too long to quote here, but the beginning will give an idea of the kind of hymn it is:

> At the cross her station keeping,
>
> stood the mournful mother weeping,
>
> close to Jesus to the last.[16]

There is another prayer, less used, called the *Stabat Mater Speciosa*, which describes Mary's feelings at the manger.

|+| The *Angelus* (fourteenth to sixteenth century). In his *Marialis Cultus* Pope Paul VI urged Catholics to say the Angelus three times a day.[17]

V. The angel of the Lord declared unto Mary,

R. And she conceived of the Holy Spirit.

> *Hail Mary,...*

V. Behold the handmaid of the Lord.

R. Be it done unto me according to Thy word.

> *Hail Mary,...*

V. And the Word was made flesh,

R. And dwelt among us.

> *Hail Mary,...*

V. Pray for us, O holy Mother of God,

R. That we may be made worthy of the promises of Christ.

Let us pray. Pour forth, we beseech You, O Lord, Your grace into our hearts, that we, to whom the Incarnation of Christ your Son was made known by the message of an angel, may by His passion and cross be brought to the glory of His resurrection. Through the same Jesus Christ our Lord. Amen.

In *Marialis Cultus* Paul VI allowed the use of the opening prayer for the Feast of the Annunciation to be used as the closing prayer for the Angelus. This is:

God our Father,
your Word became man and was born of the Virgin Mary.
May we become more like Jesus Christ,
whom we acknowledge as our redeemer, God and man.[18]

|+| *Litany of Loreto* (fifteenth century). This is a long prayer, too long to quote here (but easily available in several versions on the Web), that begins with a long list of Marian titles—like "Mother of the Church," "Virgin most prudent," "Tower of David" and "Queen of Angels"—then moves to a version of the *Agnus Dei* and closes with a prayer to God that varies with the season.

|+| *Memorare* (fifteenth century).

Remember, O most gracious Virgin Mary, that never was it known
that anyone who fled to your protection, implored your help or sought your intercession was left unaided.
Inspired by this confidence, I fly to you, O Virgin of virgins, my Mother.
To you do I come, before you I stand, sinful and sorrowful. O Mother of the Word Incarnate, despise not my petitions, but in your mercy hear and answer me. Amen.

|+| *Hail Mary* (sixteenth century). The first part is taken from the angel's greeting to Our Lady. It may have been prayed in the first century; it was used as an entrance antiphon of the Mass in the sixth century. The second part began to be used in the fifteenth century. The two were put together in the next century.

> Hail Mary, full of grace, the Lord is with thee.
> Blessed art thou among women, and blessed is the fruit of
>   thy womb, Jesus.
> Holy Mary, Mother of God, pray for us sinners
>   now and at the hour of our death. Amen.

|+| *The Fatima Prayer* (early twentieth century). Given by Mary to the three children to whom she appeared in Fatima in 1917, this short prayer is often said at the end of the rosary.

> O my Jesus, forgive us our sins, save us from the fires of
> Hell, lead all souls to Heaven, especially those in most need
> of your mercy. Amen.

What does the Church do about alleged apparitions of Mary?
The local bishop might study a reported apparition carefully, though he might not. If he does, he may declare it supernatural or not supernatural, though he may leave the matter open if the evidence is not clear. He may also approve prayer and devotion at the site of the apparition without deciding whether it is supernatural.

A word about terminology: *Apparition* is the traditional word, but *appearance* is a better word to use today, especially in speaking to non-Catholics. *Apparition* now means "ghost," and the people to whom Mary appeared saw the assumed, that is, the bodily, Mary and not a spirit.

How does a bishop decide whether Mary actually appeared to someone?

Two ways, broadly speaking.

One is by looking at the evidence as anyone would: Are the witnesses reliable? Do they have anything to gain? Is there external evidence, like miracles? Is the event producing good fruit or bad?

The other is by discerning the message: Does it conform to what God has already told us? Does it lead us to God? Does it encourage us to love and serve Him more?

The Church's standards for conviction in such matters are very high. "Probably real" is not good enough.

Do I have to believe in an apparition if the Church approves of it?

As the American bishops have explained, apparitions are a form of private revelation, and no one is required to believe in another's private revelation, even when it has been accepted around the world and included in the Church calendar. You are not required to believe in private revelations or use the devotions that grow from them, even if the Church canonizes the persons who had them.[19]

But the matter isn't entirely your own to decide. If an apparition is approved, you cannot deny it or put it down. If the Church rules against it, you cannot believe it. (Many cases the Church leaves open, but far fewer have been approved than have been denied.)

Why does Mary appear?

The obvious answer is that the message she brings is one God really intends for us to hear, and so He sends the Church's greatest member, the one who is "higher than the cherubim, more glorious than the seraphim," as the old hymn puts it.[20] Another obvious answer is that as the Mother of the Church, Mary has a special motherly desire to correct and encourage her children.

Her appearances are, at any rate, a great mercy and kindness. They are reminders that God has not forgotten us nor left us alone. They also remind us of who Jesus is and what He did for us in becoming man and accepting a horrific death—crucifixion was painful enough, but Jesus died with all our sins upon Him—and rising again. This is the mother from whom He took our nature that He might save us. She reminds us that He did so and shows us what in His grace we too can become.

Of what is Mary a patron saint?

Not surprisingly, a very, very long list of dioceses, religious orders, places, people, occupations and needs, not to mention the hundreds or thousands of churches dedicated to her.

Just in America, Mary is the patroness of the archdioceses of Atlanta, Baltimore, Chicago, Denver, Kansas City, Miami, Mobile, New Orleans, Philadelphia, Portland (Oregon) and Seattle and over sixty dioceses. The list of archdioceses and dioceses around the world is, of course, much longer. It includes, to give a representative selection, the archdioceses of Guadalajara (Mexico), Dhaka (Bangladesh), Zamboanga (the Philippines), Cologne (Germany), Pondicherry (India) and Sydney (Australia).

Many countries have taken Mary as their patron, including almost all the countries of Central and South America and all three countries in North America, the traditionally Catholic countries of Europe, plus Albania, Algeria, Arabia, Australia, China, England, Estonia, Gambia, Greece, India, Japan, Korea, Lebanon, Nigeria, Sri Lanka, Switzerland, Tanzania, Uganda and Vietnam. Mary is the patron of the continent of Africa.

Among the occupations of which the Blessed Virgin is a patron are fish dealers, aircraft pilots and air crews; construction workers; cooks; coffeehouse owners; the makers of pins, ribbon, lamps, barrels and harnesses; distillers; and Spanish architects and Spanish policemen (but not those of other countries, apparently). Perhaps unexpectedly, she is the patron of several militaries, including the armies of Argentina, Ecuador and Chile, the air force of Argentina and the navies of Bolivia and Chile, as well as the Venezuelan National Guard and the Andorran Security Forces.

Mary also serves as the patron for many needs and desires, as one would expect of someone with titles like "Our Lady of Mercy" and "Our Lady, Help of Sinners." Among the needy who call on her are the sick and those in childbirth. She also is the patron for those threatened by storms, flooding, lightning and epidemics.

Mary is, fittingly, a patron of motherhood, nuns and virgins. And enlightenment.

Isn't Mary America's patron saint?

Yes, under the title of Our Lady of the Immaculate Conception. Our bishops chose her as our country's patron at the Sixth

Council of Baltimore (then the meeting of all the American bishops, when the bishop farthest west was that of Dubuque) in 1846—eight years before Pope Pius IX declared the Immaculate Conception a dogma of the Church. The bishops' decree read:

> We take this occasion, brethren, to communicate to you the determination, unanimously adopted by us [that is, the twenty-three bishops], to place ourselves, and all entrusted to our charge throughout the United States under the special patronage of the holy Mother of God, whose Immaculate Conception is venerated by the piety of the faithful throughout the Catholic Church.[21]

They asked the pope to approve their choice, and Pius IX approved it the next year.

The American bishops also asked the pope to approve their adding the word *immaculate* to the office and the Mass for the Feast of the Conception of the Blessed Virgin Mary. They also requested an addition to the Litany of the Blessed Virgin Mary: "Queen, conceived without sin, pray for us." The pope approved these requests.

American Catholics seem always to have had a great devotion to Mary. As it happens, the first American bishop, John Carroll, chose Mary as the patron of his diocese, effectively the whole country, when he became bishop in 1790. "[Y]ou are placed ... under Her powerful protection," he wrote his people in his first pastoral letter in 1792, "and it becomes your duty to be careful to deserve its continuance by a zealous imitation of Her virtues, and reliance on Her motherly superintendence."[22]

Our Lady of the Immaculate Conception was already the patron of the parts of the country that had once been Spanish possessions. One historian estimates that of the eight-hundred-some churches in America in 1862, 145 were named for the Immaculate Conception.

Mary's patronal feast day is the Feast of the Immaculate Conception, on December 8. It is a holy day of obligation in the United States.

Isn't Our Lady of Guadalupe the patron saint of America?

Mary is the patron saint of the Americas (plural) under the title of Our Lady of Guadalupe. Mary appeared in 1531, just a few years after the Spanish had conquered Mexico, to a poor Aztec named Juan Diego, speaking to him in his own language. This was Mary's first series of appearances (at least the first we know about) in North America. She revealed herself as "the ever-virgin Mary, Mother of the true God." The appearances were accompanied by miracles, including the imprint of her image on Juan Diego's cape. She told him that a church should be built on the site of her appearances. Reportedly, millions of Indians were converted very soon afterward.

The appearances included several important symbols. The image on Juan Diego's cape wears a cincture or belt indicating that Mary is pregnant. The place of the apparitions, thought to have been the site of a pagan temple dedicated to the mother of a pagan god, made a statement about the arrival of the true God. It has been said that *Guadalupe* is a mistranslation of an Aztec word meaning "one who treads on snakes," which would be an allusion to God's description of the woman whose son would crush the serpent's head (see Genesis 3:15).

The Shrine of Our Lady of Guadalupe is the most popular shrine in the Americas. Pope John Paul II is said to have told a group of workers during his visit to Mexico in 1979, "Someone recently told me that 96 out of 100 Mexicans are Catholic but 100 out of 100 are Guadalupeans!"[23] In the United States the Feast of Our Lady of Guadalupe is celebrated on December 12.

FURTHER READING

The mystery of Mary is so intimately related to the rest of Christian revelation that a document treating almost any matter will address Mary at some point. If it talks about the Church, there will be Mary; if it talks about our Lord, there will be Mary; if it talks about Scripture, there will be Mary.

But that said, the Church has presented a great deal of teaching directly on Mary and her place in our salvation, especially in the last 150 years. Here is what could be called "the long weekend reading plan" of Scripture and of modern magisterial statements, which can easily be read and carefully studied over three days and offers a surprisingly complete introduction to Catholic belief about the Mother of God. The plan covers both Sacred Scripture and Sacred Tradition.

Almost every source in this list is easily available on the Web, often in many places. We have the Vatican Web site (www.vatican.va) and Papal Encyclicals Online (www. papalencyclicals. net). In fact, the only source not available online is the American bishops' pastoral letter, but that can be found in many Catholic bookshops or ordered from the Web site of the United States Conference of Catholic Bishops (www.usccb.org).

THE LONG WEEKEND READING PLAN

Begin by reading all the New Testament passages referring to Mary and the Old Testament passages that the Church has taken as signs or images or types of her. (Some examples are given in chapter two.) Read them with a good study Bible, tracing all the cross-references and reading all the footnotes. Two good study Bibles are the *Ignatius Catholic Study Bible* (Ignatius) and *The Navarre Bible* (Scepter).

You might also read the Second Vatican Council's Dogmatic Constitution on Divine Revelation, *Dei Verbum* (1965). This would be especially helpful in understanding how the Church developed her understanding of Mary on what is apparently a sparse foundation for so extensive a teaching.

Having mastered (well, at least read) the biblical evidence, begin the doctrinal reading. The following three documents will give a good introduction to the Church's understanding of the Blessed Virgin Mary:

· Read the eighth chapter of the Second Vatican Council's Dogmatic Constitution on the Church, *Lumen Gentium* (1964). The chapter is titled "The Blessed Virgin Mary, Mother of God, in the Mystery of Christ and the Church." (It would be best to read the whole Constitution, the better to see Mary's place in it, and because it is well worth reading on its own, but at least read the eighth chapter, which is a very good summary about Mary.) Look up each biblical reference, and read it in the context of *Lumen Gentium*'s use of it.

· Next read the 1973 pastoral letter by the American bishops, *Behold Your Mother: Woman of Faith*. It covers some of the same material as the eighth chapter of *Lumen Gentium* but puts it differently and perhaps more accessibly, and it covers devotional and other practical matters more fully, including the relation of Marian devotion and pastoral practice to the priesthood, the religious life, the family, women, youth and single people. Look up each biblical reference and each reference to *Lumen Gentium*.

· Then read through all the references to Mary in the *Catechism of the Catholic Church*, as given in the index under "Mary." It would be best to read these references in the context of the passages in which they appear. The meaning of the section on Mary in the Creed (numbers 484 to 511), for example, is illuminated by the previous description of Christ (numbers 430 to 483). As with the first two documents, look up all the references in Scripture and the documents of the Second Vatican Council.

Next turn to the papal statements on the definitions of the Immaculate Conception and the Assumption, both of which bring the general teaching to a point in a particular dogma. They are also useful to read because many of the Church's critics attack the dogmas but get them wrong, and knowing what the statements really say helps one respond. Both also quote a good many historical sources, which at least provide some knowledge of who are the major Marian theologians and a quick introduction to what they said and how they thought about Mary.

Issued in 1854, Pope Pius IX's Apostolic Constitution *Ineffabilis Deus* declares Mary free "from all stain of original sin."[1] In defining the Immaculate Conception, the pope gives a helpful review of the Church's understanding of Mary, original sin and the work of Christ.

Issued in 1950, Pope Pius XII's Apostolic Constitution *Munificentissimus Deus* declares that at the end of her life Mary "was assumed body and soul into heavenly glory."[2] In defining the Assumption, the pope gives another helpful review of the Church's understanding of Mary, original sin and the work of Christ.

You might go on to read a selection of magisterial documents. I found most useful the ones written by popes in the twentieth century and particularly after the Second Vatican Council, not because I deny the wisdom of the past but because the magisterium has gathered, summarized and refined the teaching of the past and brought it to the modern reader in a way we can more easily understand.

The average reader is safer beginning with the later documents, for the same reason he is safer beginning with a high school physics textbook and not the works of Aristotle, Newton and Einstein. But the reader will find many earlier works not only helpful but accessible. Pope Leo XIII, for example, reigning at the end of the nineteenth century, wrote many times on the rosary and once on devotion to Saint Joseph.

Ad Diem Illum Laetissimum, Pope Saint Pius X's Encyclical Letter on the Immaculate Conception (1904).

Ad Caeli Reginam, Pope Pius XII's Encyclical Letter on Proclaiming the Queenship of Mary (1954).

Marialis Cultus, Pope Paul VI's Apostolic Exhortation for the Right Ordering and Development of Devotion to the Blessed Virgin Mary (1974).

Redemptoris Custos, Pope John Paul II's Apostolic Exhortation On the Person and Work of Saint Joseph in the Life of Christ and of the Church (1989).

Redemptoris Mater, Pope John Paul II's Encyclical Letter on the Blessed Virgin Mary in the Life of the Pilgrim Church (1987).

Rosarium Virginis Mariae, Pope John Paul II's Apostolic Exhortation on the Most Holy Rosary (2002).

Readers can finish with one or more of several helpful documents:

Popular Devotional Practice: Basic Questions and Answers, by the United States Conference of Catholic Bishops (2003).[3] This short paper will help you understand the place of Marian devotion in the Christian life.

The Message of Fatima (2000), by the Congregation for the Doctrine of the Faith.[4] This short book, signed by then-Cardinal Joseph Ratzinger, explains what the Church thinks of private revelations and how their reality and value are discerned.

The Mother of the Lord: Memory, Presence, Hope (2000), by the Pontifical International Marian Academy. This book gives a clear survey of the "state of play" in the Church's thinking about Mary. It is a clear study but one aimed at more serious Mariologists.

OTHER RESOURCES

In addition to the works listed in the "long weekend reading plan," here are some books and Web sites that tell more about the Mother of God and her place in our lives. Starred books are those I particularly recommend, especially for someone just coming to know Mary.

Let me stress that this is *only* a sampling of books I've read and can commend. There are hundreds and probably thousands of worthy books on Mary, covering many levels of interest.

INTRODUCTIONS AND DICTIONARIES

Daniel-Rops, Henri. *The Book of Mary*. New York: Image, 1963. A good comprehensive introduction, with the helpful addition of the texts of several apocryphal works on Mary, including the *Protoevangelium of James*, otherwise hard to find.

Dictionary of Mary. New Jersey: Catholic Book, 1997. In addition to a comprehensive set of articles on Mary, this book offers a set of useful appendices, including a timeline of the development of the cult of Mary in the Roman liturgy and classic prayers to Mary by the saints.

* *Essential Mary Handbook: A Summary of Beliefs, Devotions and Prayers*. Liguori, Mo.: Ligouri, 1999. A very useful handbook, beginning with an exposition of Mary in Scripture, history and liturgy, and ending with chapters giving the texts of Marian prayers, devotions and shrines and a glossary of Marian terms.

Jelly, Frederick M. *Madonna: Mary in the Catholic Tradition*. Huntingdon, Ind.: Our Sunday Visitor, 1986. A comprehensive introduction to Mary, somewhat doctrinally oriented. It would be starred if it weren't out of print.

* Miravalle, Mark. *Introduction to Mary: The Heart of Marian Doctrine and Devotion*. Goleta, Calif.: Queenship, 2006. A comprehensive introduction to Mary and her place in the Church's life, doctrine and devotion, by a Mariologist teaching at the Franciscan University of Steubenville. His *Meet Mary: Getting to Know the Mother of God* (Sophia Institute, 2007) gives a shorter and simpler introduction.

MARY IN THE BIBLE AND CATHOLIC DOCTRINE

Crichton, J.D. *Our Lady in the Liturgy*. Collegeville, Minn.: Liturgical, 1997. This book explains the history and meaning of the Marian feasts, major and minor.

Gambero, Luigi. *Mary and the Fathers of the Church: The Blessed Virgin Mary in Patristic Thought*. San Francisco: Ignatius, 1991. A long survey of the development of Marian understanding and devotion in the Church's early centuries, usefully illustrated with many quotations.

* Hahn, Scott. *Hail, Holy Queen: The Mother of God in the Word of God*. New York: Doubleday, 2001. A study of Mary's place in Scripture—a far greater one than may appear at first—which conveys a great deal of learning in a very popular way.

Longenecker, Dwight, and David Gustafson. *Mary: A Catholic-Evangelical Debate*. Grand Rapids: Brazos, 2003. This respectful but pointed exchange between a Catholic and an evangelical Protestant nicely illustrates the differences between

Catholicism and traditional Protestantism and the depth and coherence of the Catholic belief.

Mateo, Father. *Refuting the Attack on Mary: A Defense of Marian Doctrine*. San Diego: Catholic Answers, 1999. A short book giving sound and useable answers to the objections often raised by Evangelicals and others.

Pelikan, Jaroslav. *Mary Through the Centuries: Her Place in the History of Culture*. New Haven: Yale University Press, 1996. Not a specifically Catholic book (the author was a convert to Orthodoxy from Lutheranism) but one dominated by Catholic writers. It gives a clear and insightful understanding of the way Christians (and others, like Muslims) have thought of Mary through the centuries and how this thinking has changed our culture.

* Rahner, Hugo. *Our Lady and the Church*. Bethesda, Md.: Zaccheus, 2004. This book reflects on Mary as our mother and the Mother of the Church, through an extensive reading of the Church fathers. Then-Cardinal Joseph Ratzinger called it "a marvelous book."

* Ratzinger, Joseph. *Daughter of Zion: Meditations on the Church's Marian Belief*. San Francisco: Ignatius, 1983. Beginning with a short but profound study of Mariology in the Bible, this short book reflects on Mary's place as virgin and mother and the dogmas of the Immaculate Conception and Assumption.

Saward, John. *Redeemer in the Womb: Jesus Living in Mary*. San Francisco: Ignatius, 1993. "An essay in reclamation," as the writer puts it in his introduction, of "a forgotten pearl from the treasury of revelation—the nine months of Jesus' embryonic and fetal life in Mary." A book worth wrestling with, as is its sequel, *Cradle of Redeeming Love* (Ignatius, 2002).

Stravinskas, Peter M.J., ed. *The Catholic Answer Book of Mary*. Huntington, Ind.: Our Sunday Visitor, 2000. Eighteen short essays by Catholic writers, and a few Protestants, on basic Marian doctrines. It also includes a few unusual subjects, like the relation between pagan myths and the virgin birth.

MARIAN TITLES, PRAYERS AND DEVOTIONS

Aquilina, Mike, and Regis J. Flaherty. *The How-to Book of Catholic Devotions*. Huntington, Ind.: Our Sunday Visitor, 2000. A very clear and practical book, with a section on praying with Mary.

Buono, Anthony. *The Greatest Marian Titles*. New York: Alba, 2008. An extensive explanation, rooted in Church teaching, of twenty-four Marian titles, ranging from "Advocate of Grace" to "Queen of All Hearts."

Crawford, Kerry. *Lourdes Today: A Pilgrimage to Mary's Grotto*. Cincinnati: Servant, 2008. A guide to the shrine, its history and the experience of Lourdes written from the pilgrim's perspective, which helps the reader understand the pilgrimage from the inside.

* Jansen, Gary. *The Rosary: A Journey to the Beloved*. New York: Madison Park, 2006. Another simple but thoughtful meditation, this one including practical help for praying the rosary. Beautifully illustrated.

Newman, John Henry. *The Mystic Rose*. Princeton: Scepter, 1996. A selection of Marian reflections by the greatest of English theologians since Anselm (and a convert). M.J.L.

Perrott's *Newman's Mariology* (St. Austin, 1997) gives a helpful survey and analysis.

Welborn, Amy. *Mary and the Christian Life*. Ijamsville, Md.: The Word Among Us Press, 2008. A simple but thoughtful meditation on Mary's life and its lessons for our own.

ECUMENICAL SOURCES

Allchin, A.M. *The Joy of All Creation: An Anglican Meditation on the Place of Mary*. Cambridge, Mass.: Cowley, 1984. A study of the thinking about Mary of certain Anglican writers and theologians. (The Episcopal Church is the American branch of Anglicanism.)

Macquarrie, John. *Mary for All Christians*. Grand Rapids: Eerdmans, 1990. A book by a leading Anglican theologian, who argues that the Catholic teaching, even the controversial doctrines, can be held in some form by all Christians.

McLoughlin, William, and Jill Pinnock, eds. *Mary Is for Everyone: Essays on Mary and Ecumenism*. Leominster, Mass.: Gracewing, 1997. Written by Christians from various traditions, these essays show how close divided Christians have come in their thinking about Mary and how far they have to go. The same editors have put together two more collections, *Mary for Earth and Heaven* (Gracewing, 2002) and *Mary for Time and Eternity* (Gracewing, 2008), also good.

Stacpoole, Alberic, ed. *Mary's Place in Christian Dialogue*. Wilton, Conn.: Morehouse-Barlow, 1982. A collection of papers by Catholic, Orthodox and Protestant writers of the Ecumenical Society of the Blessed Virgin Mary (www.esbvm.org).

Wright, David F., ed. *Chosen by God: Mary in Evangelical Perspective*. London: Marshall Pickering, 1989. A helpful collection, which includes an essay titled "Appreciating Mary" by Peter Toon, to whom this book is dedicated.

WEB SITES

Marylinks (www.marylinks.org). This site offers a wide and varied listing of Web sites dealing with Mary. It is a good place to start browsing.

The Mary Page (www.ewtn.com). An extensive site mixing original writings, including papal documents, with very helpful apologetic and explanatory articles.

The Mary Resources Page (http://campus.udayton.edu). A marvelous resource, provided by the Marian Library/International Marian Research Institute in Dayton, Ohio. It offers one-stop shopping for materials on Mary, including Church statements, explanations of doctrines and biblical studies.

New Advent (www.newadvent.org). This site offers the contents of *The Catholic Encyclopedia* (1917), an extraordinary (and easily searchable) resource.

The Vatican Web site (www.vatican.va). Includes many of the papal statements, especially those of the last 150 years, as well as the *Catechism* and the documents of the Second Vatican Council.

AND MORE

Among other books that could easily be included (many of these were recommended to me by friends longer in the Church than

I) are Romano Guardini's *The Rosary of Our Lady*, Caryll Houselander's *The Reed of God*, the chapter on Mary in Henri de Lubac's *The Splendor of the Church*, Hans Urs von Balthasar's *Mary for Today*, Hans Urs von Balthasar and Cardinal Joseph Ratzinger's *Mary: The Church at the Source*, John McHugh's *Mary in the New Testament*, Alexander Schmemann's *The Virgin Mary* (volume 3 of his *Celebration of Faith*), Louis Bouyer's *The Seat of Wisdom*, John J. Delaney's *A Woman Clothed With the Sun*, John Martin's *Roses, Fountains and Gold*, Fulton J. Sheen's *The World's First Love*, Saint Maximilian Kolbe's essay "Who Are You, Immaculate Conception?" in *The Kolbe Reader*, William Thomas Walsh's *Our Lady of Fatima* and John W. Lynch's *A Woman Wrapped in Silence*.

NOTES

CHAPTER ONE: THE LIFE OF MARY

1. Ambrose, *On Virginity*, bk. 3, no. 14, as quoted in "The Blessed Virgin Mary" in *The Catholic Encyclopedia*, available at: www.newadvent.org.
2. Pope John Paul II, Wednesday General Audience, May 21, 1997, nos. 3, 4, available at: www.vatican.va.
3. See Henri Daniel-Rops, *The Book of Mary* (Garden City, N.J.: Image, 1963), pp. 120–132; M. R. James, *The Apocryphal New Testament* (Oxford: Oxford University Press, 1924), pp. 38–49.
4. John Damascene, *Oratio* 6, Homily on the Nativity of the Blessed Virgin Mary, 2. Quoted by Marcellino D'Ambrosio, "St. Joachim and St. Ann," The Crossroads Initiative, available at: www.crossroadsinitiative.com.
5. National Conference of Catholic Bishops, *Behold Your Mother: A Pastoral Letter on the Blessed Virgin Mary* (Washington, D.C.: United States Catholic Conference, 1973), 24, p. 9.
6. *Lumen Gentium*, 64, in Austin Flannery, ed., *Vatican Council II: Volume 1, the Conciliar and Post Conciliar Documents*, rev. ed. (Northport, N.Y.: Costello, 1996), p. 420.
7. *Lumen Gentium*, 59, in Flannery, p. 417.
8 Pope Pius XII, *Munificentissimus Deus*, Apostolic Constitution Defining the Dogma of the Assumption, 5, 44, available at: www.vatican.va.

CHAPTER TWO: MARY IN THE BIBLE

1. *Behold Your Mother*, no. 12, p. 5.
2. Pius X, *Ad Diem Illum Laetissimum*, Encyclical on the Immaculate Conception, 24, www.vatican.va; John Paul II, *Redemptoris Mater*, Encyclical on the Blessed Virgin Mary in the Life of the Church, 24, available at: www.vatican.va; Paul VI, *Signum Magnum*, Letter

on the Blessed Virgin Mary, May 13, 1967, no. 1, available at: www.newadvent.org.

3. Justin Martyr, *Dialogue with Trypho*, chap. 100; Irenaeus, *Against Heresies*, bk. 3, chap. 22, no. 4, available at: www.ccel.org.

4. John Paul II, "Mary Is Outstanding Figure of Church," *L'Osservatore Romano*, August 13–20, 1997, p. 11, nos. 3, 2, available at: www.ewtn.com.

5. *Dei Verbum*, Dogmatic Constitution on Divine Revelation, 16, www.vatican.va.

6. *Lumen Gentium*, 55, in Flannery, p. 415.

7. John Paul II, General Audience of May 21, 1997, no. 1, www.vatican.va.

8. *Behold Your Mother*, 36, p. 13.

9. *Dei Verbum*, 9, 10, available at: www.vatican.va.

10. *Dei Verbum*, 7, 9, available at: www.vatican.va.

11. *Munificentissimus Deus*, 24, 26, available at: www.vatican.va.

12. *Munificentissimus Deus*, 39, available at: www.vatican.va.

CHAPTER THREE: MARY IN CATHOLIC DOCTRINE

1. My thanks to William Tighe for the translation.

2. Ambrose, *Expositio evangelii secundum Lucan*, chap. 2, no. 7, as quoted in Eugene LaVerdiere, "Mary," in Everett Ferguson, ed., *Encyclopedia of Early Christianity* (New York: Garland, 1997), p. 736.

3. Irenaeus, *Against Heresies*, chap. 19, no. 1; Ephrem, *Carmina Nisibena*, 27, 8, as quoted in Luigi Gambero, *Mary and the Fathers of the Church: The Blessed Virgin Mary in Patristic Thought*, Thomas Buffer, trans. (San Francisco: Ignatius, 1999), p. 109.

4. Epiphanius, *Panarion* (also called *Against Heresies*), 30, 31, as quoted in Gambero, p. 127.

5. Ephrem, *Panarion*, 70, 9, as quoted in Gambero, p. 128 n23.

6. *Munificentissimus Deus*, 41.

7. *Munificentissimus Deus*, 12.

8. Pope Pius IX, *Ubi Primum*, Encyclical on the Immaculate Conception, 6, available at: www.ewtn.com.

9. Pope Pius IX, *Ineffabilis Deus*, Apostolic Constitution on the Immaculate Conception, "The Definition," available at: www.ewtn.com.

10. *Ineffabilis Deus*, "The Definition."

11. Vatican II, *Unitatis Redintegratio*, Decree on Ecumenism, no. 3. The bishops say, "The children who are born into these Communities and who grow up believing in Christ cannot be accused of the sin involved in the separation, and the Catholic Church accepts them as brothers" (available at: www.ewtn.com).

12. *Ineffabilis Deus.*

13. Ephrem, *Carmina Nisibena*, 27, 8, as quoted in Gambero, p. 109.

14. "The Capitula of the Council," nos. 2, 6, in Philip Schaff, ed., *A Select Library of the Nicene and Post-Nicene Fathers of the Christian Church* (Grand Rapids: Eerdmans, 1979), vol. 14, p. 312, available at: www.ccel.org.

15. Augustine, "On the Creed: A Sermon to Catechumens," no. 6, in Schaff, *A Select Library*, vol. 3, p. 371.

16. Huldreich Zwingli, as quoted in Max Thurian, *Mary: Mother of all Christians* (New York: Herder & Herder, 1963), p. 76, and in "The Virgin Mary and Her Perpetual Virginity," program notes, December 12, 2004, available at: www.ourlifeinchrist.com.

17. From the March 25, 1539, entry in Luther's *Table Talk*, no. 4435, in Theodore G. Tappert and Helmet T. Lehman, eds., *Luther's Works* , vol. 54 (Philadelphia: Fortress, 1967), p. 34, and quoted in "Martin Luther on 'Clauso Utero' and 'Semper Virgo,'" available at: www.angelfire.com/ny4.

18. John Calvin, as quoted in S. Lewis Johnson, "Mary, the Saints, and Sacerdotalism," in *Roman Catholicism: Evangelical Protestants Analyze What Divides and Unites Us* (Chicago: Moody, 1994), p. 119.

19. For example, two major summaries of the period by eminent Protestant historians don't mention the subject at all. Jaroslav Pelikan (then a Lutheran) didn't in his *The Emergence of Catholic Tradition (100–600)*, nor did Henry Chadwick (an Anglican) in his *The Early Church*.

20. Ambrose, *Letters*, LXIII, no. 33, in Philip Schaff and Henry Wace, eds., *A Select Library of the Nicene and Post-Nicene Fathers of the Christian Church* (second series) (Grand Rapids: Eerdmans, 1988), vol. 11, p. 461. Saint John of Damascus alludes to this same verse in his *Exposition of the Orthodox Faith*, chap. 14, in vol. 9, p. 86.

21. Though Mark, Luke and John say that the stone was rolled away when the women arrived at the tomb, Matthew 28 depicts an earth-

quake as the women approached the tomb, caused by the angel's appearing and rolling back the stone. Jesus already had risen from the sealed tomb, and the angel opened the tomb so that the women could see it was empty (see Matthew 28:1–7).

22. Ambrose, Letter 44, to Pope Siricius, in Mary Melchior Beyenka, trans., *Saint Ambrose: Letters* (Washington, D.C.: Catholic University of America Press, 1967), in *The Fathers of the Church*, vol. 26, p. 227.

23. *Munificentissimus Deus*, 44.

24. *Munificentissimus Deus*, 47.

25. *Munificentissimus Deus*, 5, 12, 13, 24.

26. *Munificentissimus Deus*, 40.

27. *Munificentissimus Deus*, 12.

28. *Dogmatic Constitution on the Church of Christ*, 8, available at: www.ewtn.com.

29. *Dei Verbum*, 10, available at: www.vatican.va.

30. *Ineffabilis Deus*, "Testimonies of Tradition," available at: www.ewtn.com.

31. *Articles of Religion*, no. 2, available at: http://anglicansonline.org.

32. "Recovering a Protestant Mary: A Conversation With Timothy George," *Christian History and Biography*, no. 83 (2004), available at: www.ctlibrary.com.

33. *Unitatis Redintegratio*, 19, 21, in Flannery, pp. 467–468.

34. Reinhold Niebuhr, as quoted in David Scott, "In Her End, the Promise of Our Beginning," available at: www.davidscott writings.com.

35. The group is the Church Society, which is the dominant group of Evangelicals in the Church of England. The articles on Mary are available at: www.churchsociety.org.

36. For an Orthodox explanation, see David Bentley Hart's "The Myth of Schism," in Francesca Aran Murphy, ed., *Ecumenism Today* (Farnham, Surrey: Ashgate, 2008), pp. 95–120.

37. Sergius Bulgakov, *The Orthodox Church* (Crestwood, N.Y.: St Vladimir's Seminary Press, 1997), pp. 138–139.

38. Information supplied by William Tighe of Muhlenberg College's history department.

39. Hymns are quoted in "Dormition," available at: www.orthodox-wiki.org.

40. *Behold Your Mother*, nos. 110, 111, p. 41.

CHAPTER FOUR: THE FEASTS OF MARY

1. *Munificentissimus Deus*, no. 44.
2. Common of the Blessed Virgin Mary, 4, Advent Season, *St. Joseph Weekday Missal* (Totowa, N.J.: Catholic Book, 2002), vol. 1, pp. 1036–1037.
3. Common of the Blessed Virgin Mary, 1, *Missal*, vol. 1, pp. 1032–1033.
4. Morning Prayer, Common of the Blessed Virgin Mary, *Christian Prayer: The Liturgy of the Hours* (New York: Catholic Book, 1985), pp. 1372–1373.
5. Morning Prayer, Immaculate Conception, *Christian Prayer*, p. 1334.
6. *Behold Your Mother*, no. 88, p. 33.

CHAPTER FIVE: MARY'S TITLES

1. *The Catechism of the Catholic Church*, second edition (Libreria Editrice Vaticana, 2000), pp. 822–823.
2. J. Michael Miller, ed., *The Encyclicals of John Paul II* (Fort Wayne: Our Sunday Visitor, 1996), p. 997.
3. *Redemptoris Mater*, 33.
4. Paul VI, *Marialis Cultus*, Apostolic Exhortation for the Right Ordering and Development of Devotion to the Blessed Virgin Mary, 1–10, available at: www.vatican.va.
5. *Ineffabilis Deus*, "Explicit Affirmation."
6. *Lumen Gentium*, 62, in Flannery, p. 419.
7. Louis de Montfort, *Treatise on True Devotion*, no. 63, available at: www.ewtn.com.
8. See Athanasius, *On the Incarnation*, no. 54, available at: www.ccel.org.
9. Augustine, *Of Holy Virginity*, 3, in *The Works of St. Augustine*, in Schaff, *A Select Library*, vol. 3, p. 418.
10. *Lumen Gentium*, 53, in Flannery, p. 414, quoting Augustine, *De S. Virginitate*, 6.
11. *Behold Your Mother*, 71.
12. *Lumen Gentium*, 60, available at: www.vatican.va.
13. Pius XII, *Ad Caeli Reginam*, Encyclical on Proclaiming the Queenship of Mary, 8, 34, quoting Saint John Damascene, *De fide orthodoxa*, 1, 4, 14, www.newadvent.org.

14. *Lumen Gentium*, 59, in Flannery, p. 418.
15. *Lumen Gentium*, 62, in Flannery, p. 419.

CHAPTER SIX: MARIAN DEVOTIONS, PRAYERS AND APPARITIONS
1. Paul VI, "Exploring the Mystery of the Church," Address at the Close of the Third Session of the Second Vatican Ecumenical Council, November 22, 1964, http://campus.udayton.edu, and quoted in *Behold Your Mother*, 6, p. 2.
2. *Behold Your Mother*, 9, p. 3.
3. Ambrose, *On the Holy Spirit to the Emperor Gratian*, bk. 3, chap. 11, no. 80 in Schaff, *A Select Library*, vol. 10, p. 146.
4. Peter Damian, "Sermon for the Feast of Epiphany," in Patricia McNulty, trans., *St. Peter Damian: Selected Writings on the Spiritual Life*, trans. (New York: Harper, 1979), pp. 148–149, available at: http://www.archive.org.
5. Pope Paul VI, *Marialis Cultus*, 30.
6. J. Waterworth, ed., "The Council of Trent: The Twenty-Fifth Session," available at: www.history.hanover.edu.
7. *Lumen Gentium*, 50, available at: www.vatican.va, quoting *Roman Breviary*, Invitatory for the Feast of All Saints; see 2 Thessalonians 1:10.
8. *Lumen Gentium*, 67, in Flannery, p. 422.
9. *Lumen Gentium*, 66, available at: www.vatican.va.
10. Servants of Mary, Help of Christians, "Our Lady, Help of Christians," available at: www.catholictradition.org.
11. See John Paul II, *Rosarium Virginis Mariae*, available at: www.vatican.va.
12. As quoted in Pam Moran, ed., *A Marian Prayer Book: A Treasury of Prayers, Hymns, and Meditations* (Ann Arbor, Mich.: Servant, 1991), p. 243.
13. From the *Liturgia Horarum*. This translation is based on the *Roman Breviary*, Raccolta 321, available at: www.preces-latinae.org.
14. As quoted in "Prayers to the Blessed Virgin Mary," available at: www.catholictradition.org.
15. Adapted from Catholic Online, available at: www.catholic.org.
16. See *St. Joseph Weekday Missal*, vol. 2, p. 562, for full text. The hymn is an optional sequence for the Feast of Our Lady of Sorrows, September 15.

17. See *Marialis Cultus*, 41.
18. *Marialis Cultus*, 41; see note 109; opening prayer for March 25, the Feast of the Annunciation, *St. Joseph Weekday Missal* (Totowa, N.J.: Catholic Book, 2002), vol. 1, pp. 968–969.
19. *Behold Your Mother*, 99–100.
20. John Athelstan Laurie Riley, "Ye Watchers and Ye Holy Ones," available at: www.hymnsite.com.
21. American Bishops, Pastoral of 1846, quoted in *Behold Your Mother*, appendix, p. 54.
22. John Carroll, Pastoral of 1792, quoted in *Behold Your Mother*, appendix, p. 54.
23. Quoted in "Nuestra Señora de Guadalupe" (San Juan Capistrano, Calif.: Christian Research Institute, 1994), available at: www.sewanee.edu.

APPENDIX: FURTHER READING
1. Pope Pius IX, *Ineffabilis Deus*, "The Definition."
2. Pope Pius XII, *Munificentissimus Deus*, 44.
3. This is available at the bishops' Web site, www.usccb.org.
4. This is available at the Vatican Web site, www.vatican.va.